199 Time-Waster Situations and How to Avoid Them

199 Time-Waster Situations and How to Avoid Them

Helpful tips for people moving up the ladder of success

By Professor William J. Bond

FELL PUBLISHERS, INC.
Hollywood, Florida

AA23544

This publication is designed to provide accurate and authoritative information in regard to the subject matter covered. It is sold with the understanding that the publisher is not engaged in rendering legal, accounting, or other professional service. If legal advice or other expert assistance is required, the services of a competent professional person should be sought. From a Declaration of Principles jointly adopted bgy a Committee of the American Bar Association and a Committee of Publishers.

International Standard Book No. 0-8119-0036-3

Library of Congress Cataloging-in-Publication Data

Bond, William J.
199 time-waster situations and how to avoid them : learn how to manage your time wisely / by William J. Bond.
p.   cm.
ISBN 0-8119-0036-3 : $9.95
1. Time management. I. Title. II. Title: One hundred ninty-nine time waster situations and how to avoid them.
HD69.T54B65   1991
640'.043—dc20   88-83603
                                                          CIP

Acknowledgments

To my editor, Allan Taber, for his important editorial inputs, constructive ideas, and hard work to make this a better book.

To my publisher, Don Lessne, who believed in me and the book.

To my family, who offered tolerance, encouragement and support.

Dedication

This book is affectionately dedicated to those who use their most important resource: TIME.

Contents

Introduction

Everyone has the same amount of time. Everyone has 24 hours, 1,440 minutes, and 86,400 seconds each day. Some people seem to have the ability to use their time so they accomplish more, and get the big things done. The goal of this book will be to help you deal with the time-waster situations successfully, and avoid them in the future. Time-waster situations become part of your home and work life. A recent study on work productivity showed the average American worker loses twenty-five to thirty-five percent of his/her day to time-waster situations from procrastination to poor communication methods. This book will help you use your time more successfully at work. Time-waster situations continue to operate at home, and they include excessive television viewing, lack of delegation of chores, and lack of priorities. You will get to know your own time-waster situations and deal with them more successfully. The book is set up to not only describe the time-waster situation but also to offer a solution to help you deal with it promptly. Time-waster situations rob you of your valuable time and energy. A successful business owner was asked recently about the secret to success, and replied, "Intelligence is not enough; you need the energy to accomplish your goals." The information offered in this book will serve as an important tool to fight the time-wasters to save your energy. This book will be your handbook on managing your time for success. Time-management requires the ability to change your poor habits into good habits. For example, Shelia procrastinates before she begins any important job at work. She is required to write a report on the ACE Company, but instead, she is doing trivial jobs such as filing and sorting office supplies to avoid her #1 priority: the ACE Company report. By starting the report, Shelia will make an important step to the full completion of the report. The first step on any project or job is the most difficult. In my fifteen years of giving Time-Management Seminars, I found that success results when a poor habit is replaced with a good one.

At the end of every chapter in 199 *Time-waster Situations and How to Avoid Them* I will include a "Time-Waster Check Sheet" on which you can note the time-waster which gives you the most trouble; so with the help of this book, you can make the necessary adjustments to succeed. Now let's get started.

ONE

People Time-Waster Situations

The time-waster situations are all around you. From the moment you wake up in the morning until you fall asleep at night, the time-wasters try to get your attention and sap your time and energy. Successful people in all fields have one basic trait in common—the ability to use their time for high-payoff work. High-payoff work is the work necessary to give you the largest return or payoff. As you move up the ladder in your job, you will find more and more time-waster situations. To succeed, you must deal with them. In this book we will describe each time-waster situation and then offer some new ways to avoid or deal more effectively with the situation.

People are essential to your success. You need people to keep you informed, challenged, and continually growing in your job and life. Some people create time-waster situations by taking too much time, by being late, or by expecting too much help from you. Good time-management means examining these situations and managing around them. Develop relationships which

1

will allow you and others to grow and reach new heights of success.

#1 Time-Waster: The walk-in salespeople who want to sell you their latest product or service

Solution: If you permit salespeople to walk in unannounced, you will never accomplish the high-priority work. Turn them over to your purchasing agent. Bill A., a manager of a large tool manufacturing company, will only see salespeople on Thursday afternoon from 4:00 P.M. until 6:00 P.M. The new idea took some time to work, but now he finds much more time to do the things he needs to do to move in his career.

#2 Time-Waster: Helping your assistants too often, too much

Solution: In a recent time-management seminar, Fred D. of Connecticut, a sales manager for a large answering equipment firm, remarked at the end of the seminar, "I'm going to have a meeting with my assistant, and force her to do more of the things I hired her to do. I'm spending too much time helping her do routine work, while the large jobs are waiting in my in-box." The time-management seminar had forced Fred to examine where he was spending the bulk of his time.

Although training others helps them to grow, you must expect your assistants to quickly assume the routine work and also take on work that will help your department or organization succeed. After the seminar, Fred D. met with his assistant, Carol S. to outline the projects he expected in the next month and inform her that he would not be available in a permanent helping situation. Fred and Carol now meet each Monday morning, discuss the priorities of the department for the week, and mutually agree on responsibilities and expected completion times.

Fred now feels he can do the work necessary in his job to satisfy his own boss, because he requires his assistant to do more work on her own.

#3 Time-Waster: The people late for appointments

Solution: You had set the appointment for 10:00 A.M., and the clock is showing 10:15 A.M. Joe H., the computer manager, is late again. Try this strategy to improve the punctuality of late arrivers.

Joe: Nice to see you. The programmer asked me to review a new project. Sorry I'm late.

You: So am I, Joe. I have another appointment at eleven this morning. I wanted to spend the whole hour with you. But since you're late, we'll only have half the time.

Joe: I said I was sorry. Let's get started.

You: Yes, but remember, we are both selling an important commodity to the ABC Company—our time. Let's not waste it.

Joe: Good point. I'll remember that.

You must diplomatically let people know that you respect your own time and you're not willing to let them steal it. If you find someone habitually late for appointments, cancel the appointment and fit in some new work or continue on one of your top-priority jobs. Good time managers have the ability to automatically go back to their highest priorities. Demand that people show up on time, and thank them if they do. It sets a good tone for the meeting.

#4 Time-Waster: People who will not leave when the meeting is over

Solution: Salespeople, junior executives, and managers selling their ideas or departments feel the longer they pitch the idea or product, the better their chance of success. You have a number of strategies available to you.

You: Sadie, thanks for your time. My next appointment is waiting outside the door.

You: Charlie, I am very clear on your point of view. Give me time to discuss it with others in the company.

You: (putting on your jacket, moving abruptly) Sue, I have a very important meeting. Sorry, but I must leave right now. Thanks for your time and ideas.

You: Darrell, we covered everything. Let's not waste any more precious time and energy.

When the meeting is over, the successful time manager will switch his or her energies and concentration to the next important job, disconnecting themselves from the repeaters and people who want to reinforce their positions. When the meeting is over, close the door gently if possible—abruptly if necessary—and go on to other things.

#5 Time-Waster: Taking work or assignments that belong to others

Solution: Tim O. is office manager of a large oil refinery; and since he knows a lot about a lot of things, people from other departments line up around his desk with various jobs they should be handling themselves. But they know Tim won't let them down. They heard it over and over again: "If you don't want to do it, give it to Tim." He built a fine reputation for doing things for other people, but his own work was piling up while he worked on unrelated jobs.

Tim finally decided to ask people to come back after working hours. His own work took the high-priority, and he could only see people after 6:00 P.M. The line in front of his desk started to dwindle to the point that now only an occasional person comes in to try to give him work they should be responsible for themself. Tim O. is now doing the work he was hired to do.

#6 Time-Waster: The office pest who wants to tell you about his/her fishing trip or Saturday night's dinner party

Solution: The longer you permit the office pest to steal your time, the more difficult it will be to remove yourself from their grip. Social interaction is essential to the proper development of your career, but if the office pest steals your precious time, you will have little remaining in which to do the high-payoff work.

Take Frank D., an illustrator with a large Detroit advertising agency, who is working hard to become an art director. His weakness is permitting the office pest or others in the office to spend their idle time talking about all kinds of personal affairs completely unrelated to the job or the company. Frank's boss has commented on the numerous delays and the crowd around Frank's desk a good part of the day. One day the ABC Company needed an illustration for a large magazine advertisement, due at 2:00 P.M. Frank was trying to get the job out on time, but Susan T. was leaning over his desk telling him about the fishing trip scheduled for Saturday and doing her best to slow the work flow to minimum. Frank was at his wits end. He wanted to get the work out, but didn't want to be abrasive to Susan. Here's how Frank handled it:

Susan: We want to catch the large trout, so we plan on trying Moose Lake, then perhaps Frogs River if the weather is good. We have all the equipment we will need. I hope the mosquitoes are not too heavy in July.

Frank: Susan, I hope you have a good time. Listen, I really have to get busy on this illustration to meet my 2:00 P.M. deadline.

Susan: I just thought you liked fishing. Why are you so crabby today?

Frank: I like fishing but I also need my job. My illustration is my top-priority; I must finish it. Let's talk fishing at lunch sometime.

Susan: See you later. I have to see Betty.

Notice how Frank had to be very stern to get back to his work. In your own situation at work and at home, do you permit others to dominate your time, thus diluting your ability to achieve the things you want to accomplish? You can be assertively diplomatic, getting across the message that your desk is not the common meeting grounds for personal chatter and recreation. Once you stand your ground, the message will be passed to others.

#7 Time-Waster: Trying to be two places at once

Your boss is holding a meeting on direct marketing, while at the same time one of your best customers wants you to attend a meeting on computers. You would like to keep both happy, but although you're a very capable, motivated individual, you cannot physically be two places at once. There is a better way.

Solution: Ask someone in your office to attend one of the meetings for you. This accomplishes a couple of things: it permits you to be represented in two places; and it also gives you an opportunity to give additional responsibility to your new assistant. Good time managers are like farmers—they know they must cultivate the people around them to develop a team and reap the harvest in the future. Instead of trying to stretch yourself to the maximum, slow down and see what items you can delegate to others. By spreading the workload you can be more productive, doing more of the high-payoff work that counts.

#8 Time-Waster: Trying to do more than one thing at a time

The high-pressure executive or busy manager often tries to do too many jobs at the same time. Before she finishes one job, she starts another. At the end of the day, many jobs are started, but only a few are done.

Solution: Make a list of your priorities for today on the following illustration:

Illustration #1
List of Priorities
_____
_____
_____
_____

List them without consideration for immediate priority or urgency. Now that you have them listed, think about each one, and choose the highest priority in your job, your assignment, your organization. Now choose the one with the highest priority to *you*. The highest priority is not something that can be delayed or given to someone else. It is something important to you and urgent.

For a young man in Boston his top-priority was not in his work; it was to run a Little League program for his community. He would come home from work and drive over to the league to get the games going. His top-priority was to help his community.

Betty D's top-priority is to be the first woman CPA in her community; and she is presently taking courses at her local college to attain that goal. Stan M. is an insurance representative for a large national insurance carrier; he wants to become a sales leader, selling $1,000,000 worth of insurance so he can join the elite million dollar round table of insurance salespersons. Good time managers know that the #1 priority takes precedence over anything and everything. Now make a list of priorities—first, second, third, etc.

Illustration #2
List of Priorities   1. _____
                         2. _____
                         3. _____

Now that you have finished your listing of priorities, let's take a look at Stan M's list.

List of Priorities: Stan M.

1. Make 5 sales calls in Los Angeles Territory.

2. Call for appointment for next week.

3. Read information on new products/services.

4. Finish report on sales cost information.

5. Set up appointment to tune up the automobile.

Notice that Stan made his personal selling activities his #1 priority. Stan knows he must put his time and energy into the sales calls before he can move to priority #2 or #3. People who find time slipping away from them try to do too many jobs at once, often never finishing any of them. The solution is a simple one: start to work on your top-priority, and continue working on it until you finish it. Never, never move to a lower priority until you finish your #1. When the end of the day has finally arrived and you are still working on your #1 priority, that's all right— you're working on what you determined to be the most important and most urgent to you.

Set up your list of priorities each day, and start work on it. This priority program can be used at home as well. When my son has a number of things to do, I hold myself back from doing them for him. Instead, I ask him to make a list of the priorities and then began doing them. This practice gives my son some practice handling his own responsibilities and trains him to use his most important resource—his time.

#9 Time-Waster: The busywork person

Busywork is unimportant tasks and jobs with low payoff. It saps your energy and time, so you cannot handle the more important, top-priority work. Busywork may be filing papers, cleaning out the draws of your desk, doing routine paperwork, or any number of things that someone else could do or you could do when nothing else is pressing. High-priced managers and business executives are being paid much too much to spend their valuable time with busywork. You are being paid to do high-payoff work. Why let the busywork slow you down? Managers are paid to manage not to do clerical work.

Solution: One manager cuts his busywork to a minimum by putting a large sign in front of his desk: "I must do the most productive thing possible at every given moment." When he begins to do busywork as an excuse to delay the important work, he looks at his sign and drops the busywork. Janice K., a New Hampshire school teacher, sets deadlines for herself and her students to keep them directed towards the important work like completing important assignments, projects and tests.

Be willing to permit the guilt wheel to spin when you engage in busywork. Ask yourself whether or not you are getting closer to your #1 priority with your present activities. If not, terminate them and start the important items. Stop yourself from picking the lint off the desk, filing those unimportant papers, signing routine letters, or supervising employees who really don't need supervision. Instead, turn yourself into the modern time manager who reduces the number of routine tasks, and attend to the difficult decisions or projects. You will add to your value and promotability if you cut the busywork and routine jobs to the minimum.

#10 Time-Waster: Conforming to all the rules and operating procedures in your organization

The large electronic company specialized in doing paperwork, and all the middle managers, and potential managers, wrote memo after memo instead of using more efficient methods. Some managers even had large books where they filed all memorandums. This procedure had been started a number of years previously, and a number of people continued to follow it. Too much writing can become a time-waster.

Solution: Be willing to break the rules or common practices to beat the time-waster. Take Florence P., a cost accounting manager of a large electronic company; she got into the habit of writing longer and longer memorandums to people within her company. One day, when a deadline was staring her right in the face, and she was writing out memorandums, she told herself there must be a better way to handle this job. She decided to use the phone to present the information. This saved a great deal of time.

Florence also followed the rule of not taking telephone

calls. When someone called her, she would have her secretary take his number and call him back. Florence used this procedure because her boss and most people in the office used it. Florence found that this rule backfired with her. When the caller called again, Florence was in a staff meeting, and the circle went on and on. She decided that to prevent the long circle of telephone calls by taking the calls right away, unless she was doing top-priority, urgent work. She broke the basic rule of many people in her office, but doing so permitted her to save time and produce more. Review your style. Do you do things because "that's the way we do them here in ABC Company," even when it takes longer. Break the rules to improve your own time-management. More and more people will follow your ideas.

#11 Time-Waster: Not being prepared during a meeting, a phone call, or a business situation

You're on the phone with Ann V., the regional vice-president of production; she asks you about the production figures for your department during the last month. You know some of them by heart, but you're afraid you might be wrong. You need the production report filed away in the far corner of the production file. You need more time to get it, but you're afraid to tell her the information is not readily available. You say to yourself, if only I had had the information on hand before she called. You present the image of being confused, not staying on top of things.

One very successful chairman of a large automobile corporation carries five or six briefcases with him at all times; he wants to be sure he is not caught without the right information. There is no excuse for not being prepared, and the results of being unprepared are the wasting of valuable time and presenting a poor image.

Solution: Gather the essentials for the sales meeting. Make sure you know the sales figures by territory and by salesperson. Have the cost figures, so you can show the cost of making a sale. Know which items might be required for the meeting. If you don't have all the information, request it from others in your department. Don't take the full responsibility for putting all the material together; you might even delegate this job to someone on your staff. Once you plan the project well, you will not spend time looking for tools, materials, or equipment. You can start the project or meeting and finish it. If you are forced to delay the meeting, it will further increase the time-waster.

In summary, get the materials ready, even if it means gathering more materials and information than is required, so you can go on with the work at hand. One manager from Texas makes a checklist of the materials necessary for a meeting, and as he gathers them together, he checks them off the list. When the list is completed, he is ready for the meeting.

#12 Time-Waster: Worrying about how other people manage their time

Your boss is a time-waster; the other departments waste valuable time doing their job. You get irritated. Efficient people want performance, and they usually demand a great deal from themselves in order to get things done. No matter how efficient you are in your job, your success will depend on everyone working as a team to accomplish the objectives of the team. You have all you can do to manage yourself and your time, rather than worrying about all the other members of the team. By worrying about the time-management of others, you will fall into the "spreading yourself too thin" trap.

Solution: If your boss needs time-management, try to set up meetings when he/she is not too busy; try to take some work from him to help him with his workload. Suggest a time-management seminar, if you can do this in a diplomatic and subtle manner. Slide a time-management brochure into his mailbox.

Try to be a good time-management model yourself. When people observe good use of time ideas from you, they are more apt to use them.

If some of the people you work with show a need, time-management courses are given at management associations, business associations, colleges, universities, business colleges, and community colleges. Give your boss a copy of this book as a gift, or simply tell him about some of the ideas in the book. You can make an attempt to help others, but focus on your own time-management practices.

#13 Time-Waster: The Pessimist

Why permit the office pessimist to steal your time? Every office, business, and organization in the world has one or more pessimists. The pessimist wants to convert you to his theory that everything is wrong about the company; and once he does that, your time-management strategies will be tossed aside, leaving you to concentrate on the busywork and non-essential jobs. The pessimist, if you permit him, will cripple your effectiveness on the job and destroy all possibilities for promotions and opportunities for you in the future.

Solution: Don't let the pessimist take control of you. Stay clear of the pessimist, and give him as little information about you, your assignments, and projects as possible. For example, if you drop your pessimist guard, the following will result:

Pessimist: Hi, how is the ABC product doing these days? I know you started to work on it.

You: Just fine. We just finished the market plan, including the product strategy, pricing strategy, promotion strategy, and full distribution strategy.

Pessimist: That's a great deal of work, and also money. We should be spending more money in other areas of the company. This company really doesn't know what they're doing. They develop products that die in the marketplace. What a waste, real waste.

You: Sorry you feel that way. We have done a great deal of research on it. I hope it will make it.

Pessimist: It really doesn't matter. It will not make it. Most of our products fail.

Notice how the pessimist turned your positive thoughts into negative and pessimistic thoughts. You played right into his hands. By the time the pessimist finished, you lost the confrontation, hands down. Now let's look at another way you can handle this same basic conversation:

Pessimist: Hi, how is the ABC product doing these days? I know you started to work on it.

You: Pretty good; we are working on it. We're hoping for the best.

Pessimist: That's a great deal of work, and also money. We should be spending more money in other areas of the company. This company really doesn't know what they're doing. They develop products that die in the marketplace. What a waste. A real waste.

You: Sorry you feel that way. We look at this as an opportunity for success. We have many good indications for success. We're working very hard on it. I am attending a meeting on it, in about 10 minutes. Can we count on your help in case we need it? I really have to go. This meeting is my #1 priority today.

Pessimist: Yes, call on me if I can help.

Notice what happened in this case. You disarmed the pessimist by asking for his help in a diplomatic manner and forcing him into becoming a friend rather than a foe. They key here is you did not permit the pessimist to steal your time and you also incorporated his help for the future. Be willing to deal with the pessimist or avoid him completely so you can use your time to accomplish your goals.

#14 Time-Waster: The Procrastinator

Just as every office has an office pessimist, it grows and develops a hive of procrastinators to slow down the hardiest person, project, committee, or group. Don't permit the procrastinator to steal your time or slow down your progress. The procrastinator plays the role of the tollgate collector of the highway of success. In order to continue to ride the highway, you must be willing to pass the procrastinator by and go on to other things. One manager has some basic rules to beat the procrastinator in her organization:

1. Never delegate anything to the procrastinator.
2. Avoid working together with a procrastinator on projects.
3. Show the procrastinator that the fun is in doing a project and seeing it to completion.

Oftentimes the procrastinator delays projects because she feels she must do all the duties and jobs herself. Why not oil the delegation machine, and delegate some assignments to others. In other cases, the procrastinator delays because he wants to make sure the job is done to perfection. The procrastinator finds it easier to explain why a job is not complete, rather than to discipline himself to complete it successfully.

Solution: One time manager found himself on a committee

with the most notorious procrastinator in the company, and he knew he needed a strategy to get some production from the procrastinator. Let's listen:

Joe L: Congratulations, Lenny, on your assignment to the production subcommittee. We have a great deal of work to do, and only six weeks to do it in.

Procrastinator: I know it. I am so busy with my current jobs, I don't know how I will be able to squeeze in enough time for the committee.

Joe L: The committee will be very important for the success of the company. We selected the best committee possible. We certainly need your expertise and experience on the committee.

Procrastinator: Thanks for those kind words. I still don't think I can spare the time.

Joe L: Perhaps you can delegate some of your day-to-day work to Sue, your assistant, or Fred, the supervisor in your department. This will relieve you to concentrate on the committee assignment. We sure need you.

Procrastinator: Thanks. I'm not sure they could handle my job. It's an idea. Maybe I could use it. It's food for thought.

See how Joe L used the strategy of "we need you" to get the procrastinator to give some thought to making a commitment to the committee. Joe L wanted the procrastinator to think about making the commitment to the committee. He showed him that instead of delaying things, he could make something happen. Get cooperation from the procrastinator.

If you're the procrastinator, try to pick out one area in which procrastination plagues you; for example, delegation of routine work. Get busy on your #1 priority, and tell yourself that in order to stay on your top-priority, you must lighten the load by delegating to others. Visualize a meeting with your boss in a year, when you tell him about your successful completion of your #1 priorities. At the same time, you will have developed your department by assigning numerous routine jobs, so you can move up the promotion ladder.

#15 Time-Waster: Motivating the unmotivated, malcontent workers

Time managers know they cannot manage their time unless they can harness the energy of the people around them. One way to do this is to find out what is lacking in the malcontent's life, and deal with it by filling his need, so he can go on to bigger and better things.

Solution: Sometimes just taking the time to determine what is going on in the life of the malcontent or unmotivated person provides the solution. A very successful Marine officer noticed a lance corporal always playing the role of a malcontent. When the officer finally confronted the corporal, here is how the conversation went:

Officer: Where are you from Corporal?

Corporal: Philadelphia.

Officer: Oh, really. I graduated from Villanova.

Corporal: Really? I spent 12 years studying music, specializing in the violin.

Officer: Do you think a layoff would affect your ability?

Corporal: I don't know; my mother and father spent a great deal of money to buy me a quality violin, and I don't want to subject it to the hazards of Vietnam.

The officer asked the director of special services to buy a violin when he went to Hong Kong for recreation equipment. A beautiful violin and a pitch pipe appeared on the officer's field desk. The officer called for the corporal. When he saw the violin, the tears streamed down his face. He played at church services each Sunday and at gatherings and at the enlisted men's club. He became the most popular Marine in our camp and became a superb individual in every way. Not every malcontent or unmotivated person will be as easily directed as the above example, but the concept is clear: direct your interest into their lives, and try to find the key to higher productivity for that individual. Management is dealing with people, tuning them up so they can operate at the highest level of their potential.

#16 Time-Waster: The person who spins the guilt wheel

The meeting is in full swing. You suggest a new way to handle some work in your department, but your rival in purchasing suggests that the company should be doing this already. When you talk about the success of a project or idea that originated in your department, the operator of the guilt wheel asks about the long-overdue project you suggested months ago. The operator of the guilt wheel is a master at keeping you in your place and undermining your reputation with others in the company.

Solution: Don't let the guilt giver know he is getting to you. Be willing to spin the guilt wheel right back to him. In the military in basic training, we were taught to fight a rifle with another rifle, a tank with a tank, and a fighter plane with a fighter plane. Take the example of Pat C., a new book author, meeting head on with an associate.

Fred D: Pat, I just read your new book. Who wrote it for you?

Pat: Thanks for the compliment, Fred. Who read it for you?

Pat was able to handle the guilt giver with a heavy dose of humor. She wanted to put him back right into his place. A staff meeting found Fred acting himself again. Let's listen in to the conversation:

Pat: I think we should do a cost study to determine whether or not we should start a self-insurance program for our vehicles.

Fred D: Come on Pat, I thought we were doing that already. The ACME Company, the ABC Company, are already running a self-insurance program.

Pat: No, we are not doing that already. I can only do so much work. I'm working on my own #1 priorities. Since you're familiar with ACME and ABC Companies, call them for me and find out about their programs.

Fred D: I'm very busy, but I'll call them for you.

Pat: Thanks Fred. We need all the cooperation we can get to make this company work.

Notice how Pat was able to handle Fred D. when he tried to spin the guilt wheel by answering him directly and then delegating work to him. Keep your guard up to defend against the guilt wheel, and spin it right back.

#17 Time-Waster: Tolerating an employee who is wasting your time, or upsetting

you, by asking too many
questions

The clock on the wall is very important; you get upset when people continually ask you questions and delay your #1 priority. Experienced managers know that an organization's most valuable asset—human resources—does not appear on the balance sheet. It is up to you to make your people pull together, or you will end up hanging together. Let's look at a solution.

Solution: Archie V. is continually asking questions, about the organization, about his job, and about other jobs. It is getting to the point of being a major time-waster. Think it over carefully, and confront him directly.

You:	Fred, can I see you for a few moments?
Fred:	Sure. What is on your mind?
You:	Fred, this has nothing to do with your job in the traffic department; all of us here agree that you're doing an excellent job. But you're asking too many questions. For example, you spent 15 minutes with me this morning asking questions about the production audit, which has nothing to do with your job.
Fred:	Sorry you feel that way. I was just trying to find out more things about the company.
You:	That's fine. Knowledge is important, but you also must understand that other people have things to do. These are fine questions during your lunch hour, or after hours, but not during the prime hours of the job.
Fred:	I will keep that in mind in the future.

Notice that Fred was forced to re-evaluate his behavior; and when you detailed that behavior to him, *it showed you meant business. Delaying the direct confrontation only delays putting the time-waster in his place. Deal directly to save time.*

#18 Time-Waster: Employees in conflict with one another

Solution: Sammy V. must work closely with Wendy C. to put out the required paperwork for the company. Since they do not get along and rarely speak to one another, the work is slow and many times non-existent. Let's look at how you can deal with this problem.

You: Thanks for coming to this meeting, Sammy. It's nice to see you, Wendy; sit down and make yourself comfortable.

Sammy: Cooperation is what this meeting is all about.

Wendy: What do you mean by that. We try to cooperate.

You: Trying is not enough. We must cooperate in order to make the company work. Everyone has some differences with others, but to succeed, you must put them aside.

I am going to give you two weeks to get together. If you are not getting along better in two weeks, we will have another session. If either of you wants to see me during that period, do not hesitate to do so. My door is always open.

I don't know what the problem is between you, and I don't plan to get into it, but I ask both of you to put your differences aside and work together for the benefit of the company.

Wendy: That sounds fair to me. Let's try it.

Sammy: It's all right with me. I'm for it.

You: Thanks for your cooperation; let's make this our last meeting.

Be willing to move into a conflict situation which might interrupt the normal operations of the company. When the conflict affects your performance or cuts into profits, be willing to take the necessary action.

#19 Time-Waster: The purchasing agent or potential customer who keeps you waiting too long

Solution: One time manager puts a fifteen-minute limit on his waiting; another uses 25-minutes limit. Stick to it. Why let him/her steal your time? Make a new appointment for another time, and leave. If the appointment concerns an urgent matter, telephone later.

Try to use this waiting time as productively as possible: review the sales presentation, ask yourself about the benefits of your product or service, visualize in your mind a successful meeting and a signed contract, handle any routine tasks, review tomorrow's list and all appointments. One salesman uses waiting time to make phone calls to set up other sales appointments. At the end of the meeting, call ahead to confirm your next appointment.

Review Illustration 3, and list any time-waster situation which you would like to change from a problem into an opportunity to succeed in the time-management game. You manage your time and your life. A "Time-Waster Check Sheet" will be offered at the end of each chapter for your convenience. Use it.

Illustration #3

Time-Waster Check Sheet

Date	Time-Waster	Solution	Remarks

TWO

Machine Time-Waster Situations

"Machines are made by man to save time for even more enjoyable things"

Bill Bond

Today's business office is filled with computer terminals, calculators, automated telephone systems, electronic message systems and fax machines. Just as time managers control people time-waster situations, they control and manage their machines as well. Your machines are tools, and used properly they can cut your work and give you more time. Don't permit your machines to manage you, keep your machines working to reach your goals.

Think of your machines as important resources to do your job better. For example, Elevyn M. of Florida, is assistant manager of a large maintenance organization. Her boss assigned the full accounting duties to her last month. Elevyn was forced to learn the full systems, and use them in all the accounting areas. To make things easier, she called each system a different name, and developed the ability to discuss the system's role in easy to understand terms. For example, one system she calls "Fred" includes all contract and agreements with customers, and the second system, "Dolly," includes all the invoices billed to customers, the third system called "Charlie," includes how much her customers owe her company. Elevyn depends on Fred, Dolly, and Charlie to do her job better, saving time, money and effort. Use every resource possible.

#20 Time-Waster: Too many telephone calls

Your telephone is always ringing off the hook. When it finally slows down, you're placing calls to people you missed, salespeople, associates, classmates, golf friends, association members, etc. At night you dream of talking over the phone.

Solution :   A time manager from Vermont found he was spending too much time on the telephone. He went to a time-management seminar and came back with a large sign that he put next to his telephone. The sign says:

1. Think before you dial.

2. Delegate the low-priority call to your assistant, your secretary, or the person in your office that can answer the calls.

3. Learn to say, "Sorry, but I have someone waiting for me.... Goodby."

One manager solves the problem by leaving precise messages with secretaries and assistants when he has trouble reaching his callers. Why continue to recall and recall, when a short message can do the job.

When you leave precise messages, make certain the messages are favorable ones. There is nothing more demeaning than receiving a message that is unfavorably delivered by an assistant or a secretary. For example, your secretary saying, "Bill called; the sale went to Sue's company." Also, in jobs such as sales, telemarketing, personnel, and human relations you should accept the fact that numerous calls are required. Continue to ask yourself if the call is necessary; when the call is completed then go on to the other things.

#21 Time-Waster: Spending too much time looking up telephone numbers

You talk with about 25 different people each week. You cannot remember all the numbers, so you spend time looking them up in your rolodex or large phone directory. At the end of the day, you have spent a large chunk of time looking up these numbers.

Solution: Get your own personal telephone book and list the most common calls in this book, alphabetically, to cut wasted time to a minimum. An accountant from Ohio made his personal phone book fifteen years ago in his first job. When he got promoted to another company, he took the book along with him. He is on his fifth job now, and he uses the same book, with all his contacts in tact. The book includes the caller's title, department name, etc.

Another successful time manager from Alabama uses his appointment book, which has a separate page on which he lists the names, addresses and phone numbers (both home and business) of the 25 more common calls—his customers, associates at work, people he deals with on a daily basis.

The telephone company also has a special telephone system, called *Speed Dialing* where you only have to punch one or two digits of commonly called numbers, instead of the entire number. Talk with your local telephone customer service department to design a telephone system that meets your specific needs.

#22 Time-Waster: I miss people; when I call they are out, in meetings, not available right now, etc.

This is a very common time-waster in both time and money. When you call long distance, and your party is unavailable, you still pay for the call, and you're left without an answer.

Solution: Be willing to ask for your party's assistant. If the party is unavailable, ask your questions to the assistant. If the assistant cannot assist you, leave a precise message and an exact time when you will be available. Another technique is to call your party at a time when they will be able to take your call. For some busy people it is early or late in the day; once the normal hectic day starts, it offers little time for phone calls. Office productivity studies shows the high peak to be around eleven o'clock in the morning. This is not the best time to try to get someone on the telephone. Lee M. of New Hampshire uses a telephone appointment method to reach people. She drops a post card in the mail and tells them she wants to set up a phone appointment for say ten A.M. on July 7th. Unless she hears from her party, she goes ahead with the phone call at the scheduled time.

Save money by calling your difficult to reach party person-to-person. The operator will help you get Sue Jones, Manager of Personnel, and you will not be billed until she is on the line. If the operator cannot reach her, he or she will tell you when Sue will return to her desk or office, and when you can expect to reach her. A salesperson from Minnesota uses this technique to inform purchasing people that he will be making a special trip to their area during the coming week. This special person-to-person call shows his interest in the purchaser and heightens the anticipation of the future meeting. Let's listen to the call:

Polly: How are you, Oscar? Is it hot enough for you? It is very nice to speak to you. I am making a special trip to Chicago next Friday; I want to confirm our appointment. I have the C-100 computer terminal you wanted to see. This terminal is everything you read about in our national advertising.

Oscar: Good. Why did you call person-to-person?

Polly: Because you're a special customer. We appreciate your business.

Oscar: I would like to see it. Thanks for the special call.

Polly: I look forward to seeing you again.

Even when you miss your party on the telephone, always leave your name and number. When your party returns to his office, your name will force him to think about you, and increase your chances of getting a return call. You may be competing with ten or twenty other callers, so when you just call without leaving your name, number, and reason for call, you will weaken your chance to connect to your party.

#23 Time-Waster: Failing to use your computer

Six months ago Tom M. purchased a personal computer to help him deal with the large pile of paperwork in his training department. He still has not cut his manual work any—or the dust from the top of his computer.

Solution: Tom M. decided to make a list of the reasons why he purchased the computer in the first place. Reviewing the reasons forced him to use it. For example, here are just a few ways Tom could use the computer to help him do his job better:

1. Revising, writing and storing manuals.
2. Designing, scoring and analyzing surveys.
3. Record keeping.
4. Instructor tracking.
5. Cost/benefit calculations.
6. Research.

When the computer is used as an important tool in your office or organization, it can save you a great deal of time, money and effort. The computer was purchased to be used, and it will be up to you to use the machine to help you do your job.

When do you decide on a computer? As a general rule, you must compare the cost of performing certain functions by hand to the cost when you computerize the operations. If you can save money by using the computer, use it. Why let your competitor beat you to the punch. The computer can be the tool you need to eat up the jobs that eat up days of time and to deliver information you need to succeed.

#24-Time-Waster: Not using toll free 800 numbers

If you purchase products or services, consider using the toll free 800 numbers. a directory is available at your local book store for as little as $3.85. More and more companies are installing the 800 numbers to increase their sales. A potential customer with a question might not write a long letter to the seller but would call if the call is free. When you use the 800 number, you will receive excellent service.

Solution: Use the 800 numbers, because time will be saved. If you're not sure whether a company has an 800 number, call

800 information, by dialing 800-555-1212, and they will look the number up for you. Include the 800 number in your personal telephone book, so that you can use it again in the future. Use 800 numbers—they work for you.

#25 Time-Waster: Calling a difficult-to-reach executive long distance; and finding her unavailable or out of the office

Time-management studies have shown that the telephone is one of the most disruptive, difficult-to-control devices in an office, and very expensive as well. For example, if you missed making a long distance connection with someone four times per week, at an average cost of $2.00 a miss, that's over $400 per year, plus your time and effort making these calls.

Solution: Call the difficult to reach person at a special time in the day when she is most likely to take your call. Sometimes early in the morning or late in the afternoon is effective. Some successful time managers make telephone appointments to make sure they will get their part.

A successful time manager from Wyoming, calls her difficult to reach people person-to-person. When the party is not in the office, she saves the money it would cost her if she had not called person-to-person. By using the person-to-person method, she can leave word for her party, and when they call back, she can accept the charges once she is connected. The important benefit of person-to-person calling is you don't have to pay anything until you get the individual, and you save time by not talking with someone else who cannot answer your question. Use the person-to-person method of calling to save time and money.

#26 Time-Waster: When the phone controls you

You're on the phone with the vice-president of Socko Company, and you get a beep from your secretary that another call is waiting from the ABC Company in Miami. Do you take the call, or do you have your secretary take your message? Who is making the decision about what calls to make, accept, delay, or reject completely?

Solution: There are machines on the market called phone organizers and instead of your secretary buzzing you about another call, she presses the send button, which flashes that message onto your display while making a very soft audible beep to attract your attention.

Now you have the choice about the call. You can tell your secretary to hold the call or take a message, or you could tell the second caller that you'll call right back—simply by pressing two buttons. You have not interrupted your phone conversation; you've communicated your wishes to your secretary; and you, not your secretary, determine the priority of your calls. Even if you're working on your 10-year report for your boss, your secretary can flash the incoming calls onto your display and you can determine whether or not you want to be interrupted. The machine also has a memory, and when you're out of the office, or during the weekend, it can take up to thirteen messages. It also can store several common requests. Simply by tapping one key, you can quickly roll through the options to the one you want. For example, "Coffee please," or "Please see me right now," or, "Please call my broker." The machine is simple to use and can be plugged right into your wall outlet.

Another way to untangle yourself from the control of the phone is to simply inform your secretary or receptionist that you will not accept any calls during the next hour. It will be up to you to weigh the benefits of taking calls versus the uninterrupted time necessary to accomplish important work.

#27 Time-Waster: The new computer or software

You want to learn all phases of your new computer. You especially want to learn the new software on automated accounting. You enjoy it but it takes too much of your time. You feel like a data entry clerk, rather than the manager or owner of the business.

Solution: Learn just enough of the computer or software so you can understand the basics and teach it to your assistant or data entry clerk. Turn the work over to your assistant, but make sure you're keeping a check on it regularly.

Get back to work on more important high-payoff work.

Illustration #4

Time-Waster Check Sheet

Date	Time-Waster	Solution	Remarks

THREE

Methods as Time-Waster Situations

Lost, yesterday, somewhere between sunrise and sunset, two golden hours, each set with sixty diamond minutes. No reward is offered, for they are gone forever.

Horrace Mann

You can get things done by using the correct methods. The successful time managers have the ability to examine fully the things they want to do and the best way to do it. For example, before you write an important letter to your customer, plan what you want to say, gather the necessary data, and then write your letter. Observe how other people at home, in your office, or organization handle certain projects and the methods they use. The correct methods permits you to work smarter, rather than work harder in your competitive world.

#28 Time-Waster: Following the Crowds

The lunch room is filled at noon, the bank is crowded on Friday evening, the roads are filled during the morning and evening commuting hours. You are following the habits of other people.

Solution: Vary your schedule. For example, take your lunch hour from 11:00 A.M. until noon to avoid waiting in line each day. Leave home earlier to beat the heavy traffic during commuting hours.

At home, by getting up earlier, you can bath, dress, and eat breakfast before other members of the family compete for the bathroom. Fill your car with gas at night so you can start your drive to work without interruption.

#29 Time-Waster: Doing heavy or difficult work yourself

Successful time managers know that only so much work can be accomplished by one person. Successful people pick the jobs they want to do, and assign certain jobs to other people.

Solution: Ask others to do the heavy work. I worked at a company recently, and a delivery truck came to the side door to deliver some packages. The boss went to the truck and asked about the packages. He carried two little boxes, the size of tie boxes, and went to someone else for help: "Paul, there is one box left; go in and get it." Paul walked into the large truck and carried out a large box the size of a king sized mattress. Paul was a big, rugged young man who enjoyed lifting things, and the boss took advantage of his ability. Ask yourself what jobs you take on yourself could be handled more easily and quickly by others in your office.

#30 Time-Waster: I forget to reschedule a definite

meeting or to check back with
a customer or associate

When the customer is very busy with the annual closing of
his accounting books, he cannot take the time to see you. If he
says to check back with him on January 15th, he does not mean
March 1st or April 5th. You need a method to remind yourself
to make the future call or meeting. Poor time managers leave
this to their poor memory or the happens chance to recall it.

Solution: Set up what is called a tickler file. Dana S., a business owner from New York, uses one to set up meetings with
her clients. For example, if on March 15th she wants to meet
with Alan S. and he is not ready to buy at that time, she puts his
name and the name of the potential product or service in her
tickle file for the 15th of April.

Tickler File
15 April 19—   Alan S. - give information
                               on product 5331

When you pick out the tickler file on April 15th to call Alan
S., put this down on your "Things to Do" (see Ill #5) list for
today. By using the tickler file in concert with the "Things to
Do" list, you will pay attention to projects that might be forgotten or handled too late to matter. This tickler file can be a real
time saver for you.

#31 Time-Waster: Standing in line making copies
or spending time looking for
papers to make copies

You need another copy of the sales letter or the publisher's
contract or the agreement with the ABC Company for the meeting on cost saving. You spend your valuable time standing in
line making copies, or you send your assistant, who should be

Illustration #5

THINGS TO DO TODAY!	Date:_____

Urgent ✓

Done ✓

☐ 1. ☐

☐ 2. ☐

☐ 3. ☐

☐ 4. ☐

☐ 5. ☐

☐ 6. ☐

☐ 7. ☐

☐ 8. ☐

☐ 9. ☐

☐ 10. ☐

NOTES:

doing more valuable things, to make some quick copies. You must not only protect your own time, but the time of your secretary or assistant as well. How can you multiply yourself with high-payoff work when you spend your time and your assistant's time with the trivial.

Solution: Set up a "Reproduction File" of originals or good copies of the papers you use regularly in your business or organization. Keep more than one copy in this file, so you can simply use one from the file when you need one. One time manager from Houston keeps the following in her "Reproduction File": promotional material, order forms, form letters, press releases and other commonly used papers. Another time manager from California groups some originals together, and at the end of the day, makes the necessary copies.

#32 Time-Waster: Concentrating your time on the daily, familiar jobs

You know you should be doing something else—the high-priority jobs you told your boss you could do when you first started the job. Now the smaller, daily jobs are strangling you. Break away from the daily routine by tricking yourself into the high-payoff or important jobs. Let's review the solution.

Solution: Break the high-payoff job into manageable parts. Let's say you want to write a report on an advertising campaign for your company. Fist develop a theme for the campaign. Once you finish the theme, you can then write some advertisements. Next, consider where you will place the advertisements, etc. Notice how you take one manageable part at a time. When you finish one part, it gives you the interest and the motivation to move to another part. When the job begins to fall into shape, you will tell others about it, and it becomes something that your cannot forget; it becomes an important part of your time-management program. The reward is doing each part and seeing it fit together like a puzzle. You're motivated to finish it. Be willing to reward yourself when you succeed. By giving yourself a reward, you have something to look forward to during your work. Some innovative companies are also using the reward methods to increase motivation and better use of time.

Diamond International developed a campaign to motivate their employees. The reward program simply involved giving points to each employee; when they acquired a certain number of points, they received a special gift. For example, if you worked for one year without using over three days sick leave, you got twenty points. Once you got 100 points you got a jacket. It may not sound like a large gift, but it served as an important feedback technique to show that the company cared about the employee. Be willing to give yourself the rewards necessary to give you the extra desire to reach for the next rung on the ladder of success.

#33 Time-Waster: Trying to determine which job is the most important

In a recent time-management seminar, I had an industrial writer for a large computer company ask this question: When you have two jobs, how do you pick the most important one? This is a relevant question. You must ask yourself a number of questions to determine which job is the most important.

Solution: One time manager from Arizona, Betty F., uses a series of questions to determine the most urgent and important job:

1. What is done?
2. Why is it done?
3. How is it accomplished?
4. Where, when, by whom.

Determine which job is going to give you the largest return on investment, and then go to work on it.

#34 Time-Waster: Trying to locate key equipment or personnel

When the construction company was small, with only a few pieces of equipment and a few employees, it was easy to keep track of the machines and employees. Now, with various engineers and supervisors visiting construction sites, difficulties arise as to who is working outside or inside the office.

Solution: Everyone in the office should know where all key employees and equipment are. If people within your office don't know where the key people are located, the word will get around that your company lacks organization. Develop a communication tool to inform everyone within your department or company. One of the best ways to do this is a large visual board. You can use one similar to the following:

Name	Job	In	Out	Out-Will Return
				8 9 10 11 12 1 2 3 4 5
W. Bond	Mt. Foot	X	X	
C. Roberti	Noon Bldg	X	X	

Equipment Location

Bell Tower	Marry Bldg	Syatt Hotel

Use the above illustrations to put yourself closer to the people and equipment in your organization. You can be closer to everything if you use better methods at work.

#35 Time-Waster: Doing things the same way

You know how to handle the routine jobs. Even the more difficult jobs, you tend to do the same way time after time.

Sometimes, the guilt wheel spins when you know you do a job the difficult way or spend more time on it then necessary.

Solution: Look at a job in a different way. Can you do it a different way? Can someone else in your office or home help? Try to classify your time into uncontrollable time and controllable time. The uncontrollable time is that part of the day in which you must get the production report out by 11 A.M. or when you must attend a meeting called by your boss. Controllable time is that part of the day in which you can make a decision on what job you want to do. You have time to think about how you want to handle this part of the day. Good time managers look carefully at how they use this controllable time, They know they only have a limited amount, so they use it to the maximum. Be willing to review how you spend the controllable time, and make an effort to use it as efficiently as possible. Once in the controllable-time period, make a list of the things to do, assign a priority to each, begin working on the most important priority, and keep working on it until you complete it.

#36 Time-Waster: Overlong lunch hours or coffee breaks

You asked Bill V. to lunch to go over the new union contract for the building trade employees. You have other work left at your desk, but time keeps moving, and the lunch is now two hours long. You tell yourself: This time is important; Bill should know about the contract, but you also wonder whether two hours is needed. Good people managers also know that time must be allotted to other areas as well. The key question here is where does the line end between being interested in others and spending excessive time.

Solution: One administrative assistant, Earline V. will set up a luncheon appointment when she feels it will be worth the time and effort. She will make a reservation at the restaurant to avoid waiting for a table and set a timetable and agenda for the luncheon. Earline limits the drinks to one order and gets down to the agenda right away. When the agenda and time for the luncheon is finished, Earline summarizes the various things covered during the luncheon and goes on to other things. She finds that people respect her time more when she becomes better at allotting it. Earline refuses to spend time dawdling over coffee breaks and lunches. She shows others she controls her time. You can do the same.

#37 Time-Waster: Fragmenting your work

You start the day doing your #1 priority. But then the phone rings, and the mail arrives, and Jones asks about the ABC Co. order, and Sue asks for a raise. You leave the #1 priority to get involved in the various other jobs; the day goes by and you never get back to your #1 priority.

Solution: Be very strict about getting back to your #1 priority, which will give you the payoff you need to be successful in your job. There will be minor interruptions all day long; you must be like the jack-in-the-box that gets back up again and again to continue on the #1 priority. If the #1 priority is to complete the "2-year plan on engineering" you must be willing to spend the necessary time. Spending too much time on unrelated jobs will not help you reach your #1 priority. Although you may find it interesting to get off the #1 priority track and start something else, you will fall further behind.

One time manager from Ohio, Joseph L., uses a large sign in front of his desk. The sign reminds him to stay on his #1 priority, to get the important things done to run his business successfully. The sign says:

"I must do the most productive thing possible at this given moment....."

Keep a folder on your desk and name it the #1 folder. When you arrive at work in the morning, go to that folder, start on that job, and work on the #1 job until you finish it. Go to the next most important job only when #1 is completed. If you fragment your work, you will never finish the most important work.

#38 Time-Waster: Not using prime time

Office productivity studies show that highest levels of productivity in various companies in the United States took place between 11:00 A.M. and 1:00 P.M., and leveled off slightly for the rest of the day.

Solution: Take an inventory of the degree of productivity at your office. What time of the day is the phone ringing? What time of the day has the greatest number of meetings? What is the busiest time of the day? This will give you an idea when people are at their maximum level of energy. Be willing to tap this energy.

Set up important appointments and meetings around 11:00 A.M. You will be dealing with people at their optimum level, and you can attain the highest productivity from them. By holding important meetings early in the morning, people might be still thinking about the weekend or the night before and unable to get into the subject of the meeting. If you hold the meeting at 5:00 P.M. you will find many of your employees or associates at the tail end of their energy; the efficiency of the meeting will be reduced. You're in control. You can choose the best possible time for you and for your successful interaction with others.

#39 Time-Waster: Inflexible in changing priorities

Your plans are all set. You want to spend your time interviewing a number of applicants for the head bookkeeper's position. This is an important position, and you want it filled so you can do the high-payoff work that is necessary to your success. High-payoff work means work which will payoff in more money or results in your job. You and your boss spend three days interviewing a number of applicants. Four of the applicants look interesting. A week has passed since you interviewed the candidates, and other problems have arisen in the office. Your main customer is complaining about his last shipment of products; he is hinting he might send them all back and do business with someone else. What do you do?

Solution: What is the high-payoff work? Naturally, the customer is the most important. Take care of the needs of your customer. Your main customer must be satisfied. Accept change. Be willing to move to the most important work for the good of the company, and also for you. If you lose the main customer, you will not need a bookkeeper, because you will lose a portion of your profits. Time managers change plans. Once you satisfy your unhappy customer, you can then go back to interviewing the remaining applicants for the bookkeeper's position. Be willing to change as circumstances change, or you will be left at the train depot without a ticket, watching the success express pulling out to the success wonderland.

#40 Time-Waster: Forgetting valuable company information

Your boss calls you in to her office. She asks you about the status of the following projects:

Fox Company Sales for month
Date of closing of Bond Building
Real estate listings in Nebraska's Office
Status of retirement party for Earl Mantem

Some of these questions can be answered from the top of your head. You're pretty sure you're right, but one or two of these questions you're really not too sure of. If you give your boss some wrong information, you will waste his time and lose his regard for you. A good manger knows that snap answers are not always correct; and successful managers know their reputation is important to them.

Solution: Be willing to tell your boss you really are not sure and you need a little time to check it out. It will be much better to look it up then give the information and be sorry about it. Your work style can show your confidence or your lack of it. People will avoid you if you're wrong too often. Take the example of Rhonda C., an office manger, she keeps a long list of information that relates to her office. The log is kept close to her phone. When she needs information, she reviews it closely. By using the log, she is not forced to remember everything that goes on within her department.

Telephone Log

Date	Subject	Status
July 31	ABC Co. Contract	Needs further checking by their attorney
July 31	Sale to Farmer Co.	They want 7 days to analyze bid.

#41 Time-Waster: Excessive time reading

You want to meet the demands of your job and also be aware of new things that may be important to your job. You try to read everything within your reach. You want to stay on top, and you feel you can do this by reading every word on every sheet of paper near you.

Solution: Don't try to read every word. Preview the material you want to read first. This preview of the material is quite short. It will only take ten to fifteen minutes to know how the information is organized and what general theme the author of the book or material is delivering. Next read the material until you're filled, and then paraphrase what was just read. You can paraphrase by expressing the author's thoughts into your own words. By paraphrasing you get practice recalling information, allowing you to monitor your ability to comprehend. By stopping regularly to paraphrase, you are forced to think about what you read. The next step is to elaborate on the information— openly discuss it with another person or express your opinion of it. The key here is to take the basic material and understand it; do not read every word. Skim to the essentials.

#42 Time-Waster: Asking isolated questions, rather grouping them together

You want to ask about the purchase order on the ABC stock? You cross Susan the purchasing manager in the hall and ask her about it. You receive the answer. Later in the afternoon, you have another question, so you call Susan. You're wasting your own time as well as that of the manager.

Solution: Make a list of questions for the purchasing manager so when you finally see her you can present all the questions at once. Keep a list of the answers in case you may want to refer to it in the future.

#43 Time-Waster: Keeping the difficult jobs to yourself

Time-management studies have shown that people who keep the difficult work to themselves do so because they feel other people are not up to accomplishing the work. They feel more in control when they do the work themselves. When questions are asked about the work, they can give the answer freely and quickly.

Solution: Be willing to ask others working for you to help with the work. Give them an opportunity to accomplish more work for you. It may mean training them to take on the additional work; but you must be willing to free yourself up to handle the #1 priority that will get you the promotion, the opportunities, and the rewards within your organization. Be willing to release work to others around you, and be willing to check their performance. When they complete it correctly, let them know that the job was done correctly. Remember, doing the job for the first time is very difficult; it took you a certain amount of time to learn.

Not everyone will enjoy the additional duties you delegate. Some might even complain. Take the example of Bill B., a controller with a paper recycling company in Massachusetts. He decided he wanted to delegate more so he could handle a #1 priority, a computerized accounting system for his boss. He delegated a number of assignments to Gloria V. and Ben D., and they ran to Bill's boss to complain about the additional work. Bill and his boss came to an agreement about the amount of work that should be handled by Gloria and Ben. Bill decided it was better to over-delegate than to under-delegate work so he could reach his #1 priority. Bill learned form this experience and is very careful about the amount and type of work delegated to others around him. Try to do the same; build a team that can work together.

#44 Time-Waster: Waiting until tomorrow to start your system

You somehow get your work done on time; but by the end of the day you're dead tired. You know you're doing some things the hard way—there is an easier way—but you continue to put off the formulation of a system for your work. This time-waster can sap not only your energy, but also your opportunities for promotions and future opportunities in the organization. You will not get a second chance to give your boss a good first impression. Get your system in order.

Solution: Plan your chores for a given day. Make a list of them and then set them up into priorities. Which one is top-priority? Which one or ones can be delayed? Which ones can be dropped completely? For example: first, you want that information for that report for your boss; second, you want to plan the business meeting with the Socko Company vice-president; and third, you want to call your salespeople in the field. When one task is completed, go on to the next one. Once a system like this is in operation, it becomes your work style and an important factor your boss, supervisor, or manager may consider when reviewing your performance during the annual performance review. Other people in your office may learn something from your techniques. You become a leader in time-management and self-management, and you will continue to hone your system skills as time goes on. Develop a system and then work on it.

#45 Time-Waster: Keeping too many papers

You know you should keep your desk as clear as possible, but you permit more and more memorandums to pile up on your desk. You hope to read them when time permits, but the desk gets bulkier and bulkier.

Solution: Periodically, say once a week or every two weeks, go through the various papers and ask yourself whether you really need each sheet of paper. Will this paper help you complete your #1 priority? Will this paper help you reach your goals. Get the feeling of achievement and freedom by simply putting the useless, duplicate papers right into the wastebasket. One manager from Tennessee uses late Friday afternoons to clean up his desk of all extra papers. He puts his desk into order just like he was going on vacation. By the time he leaves his desk on Friday afternoon, he is ready for Monday with a clear desk and filing system for the most efficient operation.

#46 Time-Waster: Typing out letters over and over again

Solution: The typewriter is a tool in the office, but it is being replaced by the word processor. A recent study by the American Productivity Center (APC) in Houston shows new ideas on what makes productivity work. Thirty-five percent of the respondents said word processing was the technique that worked best. The word processor can handle the routine letter writing. One disk can be used for the basic letter, and you can automatically do as many letters as you need. The word processor can be used to keep your customer or mailing list up to date. You can produce software or purchase software to help you accomplish more and more jobs and procedures. The cost of typing, dictating, and mailing a letter is getting higher and higher each year. Consider using a word processor to save a great deal of time, effort and money in your operation.

#47 Time-Waster: Failing to use available resources

Solution: There is a gold mine of information right within your organization. This gold is in the form of information in your current files, in books and manuals in your personnel department and library, and in the people within your office or organization. Be willing to spend the time and effort to get the answers that are readily available to you. Don't make the mistake of trying to get information from your corporate office or from your division office when that information originated in your own office or plant. Why go outside your organization if you can get the information locally? Needless to say, you can waste your time and perhaps your career when you fail to use your available resources.

Another important resource available to you would be the Federal Government, which has experts in every area. Whatever product or service you sell, the Federal Government has experts available to help you in this area. They also have numerous pamphlets and manuals available free or for a nominal fee to help you in your research. Use them.

#48 Time-Waster: Giving your answers too quickly

Your boss, the vice-president of a large leather belt manufacturing company, has a habit of assigning one job to three or four subordinates, all about the same rank within the company. The boss wants to determine the market of leather belts. You're eager to please the boss and report your answer ahead of the others. Because you failed to do all the necessary homework and carefully check your answer, it is not as accurate as you would like. Your answer does not square with the facts. You get the answer back and must do the necessary work to refigure it to come out with an answer that reflects reality. You lose valuable time and gain a reputation for carelessness.

Solution: Take the necessary time to master the facts of the job. What are you trying to determine? The more you know about what you're trying to do, the easier it will be to do it. Learn as much about the subject as possible. What type of belts are you dealing with—artificial or genuine leather? Get all the information together and concentrate on quality of effort rather than speed for the answer. The boss will remember you when your answer is correct. Your reputation for getting the correct answers will help you continue to do more in the future. Quality of your answers is more important than quick response.

#49 Time-Waster: Keeping your papers in one pile

Some of the papers are important. Others are not. Some can be thrown away, others should be filed or acted upon. When someone asks you a question, you tend to look under a pile of papers to support your position. You look confused and unorganized. There is a much better way to organize and manage your papers.

Solution: Sort them right away. Try to touch each paper once. Make a decision on it. One time manager from Idaho, Carol Z., an office manager, finds that by using clothes pins, she can keep her papers organized. Each pin has one of the following words printed on it:

Bills
Hold
Important
Tomorrow

She used this method, and within a few days she had her papers under her control. When someone asked about a particular paper or question, she was able to go directly to that assigned pile of papers. This new technique saves Carol a great deal of time and effort. It could work for you as well. Keep those papers organized!

#50 Time-Waster: Lack of a daily quota

What do you want to accomplish today? Today is forever. It will not come back. Why not use it to the fullest? You can do this by setting a quota for yourself. Do you want to begin that #1 priority? Do you want to spend more time with your family or that special person?

I recently received a letter after being a guest on a radio program. The lady said her #1 priority was to do more things for herself. She wanted to do things she wanted to do and spend more time with her grandchildren. Another person wrote that since she retired, she could not find time to write and paint, her #1 priorities. There is a real need to set up a daily quota to accomplish these important things. Let's look at some ways you can set a quota for yourself that will work.

Solution: The daily quota will help you reach the weekly, the monthly, and eventually the yearly quota. There will be time in which the daily quota is not possible—an illness, an accident—but if you reach it most of the time, you will reach success. Take the example of Judith Krantz, best-selling author of *Daisy, Ministrial's Daughter* Judith sets an eight-hour quota of writing everyday, seven days a week. She avoids the traps of leaving her office at home to check the mail; and she does not take telephone calls until the end of her eight hours of writing. In my interview with her, she claims once her books start, she thinks about it at all times, even when she is in the hairdresser's chair. She continues to take notes and write her book. Judith Krantz is not only strict with herself on the daily quota for writing, but she will not reward herself for a book until it reaches the top of the best-seller list. Once it reaches the top of the list, only then will she buy something special for herself or feel herself worthy of the rewards.

Review what daily quota you will need to reach your goals; then make the effort to reach it. You can better your best. If you don't go out on a limb, on a daily basis, you will never reach the fruit. Set a quota and then go out to reach it.

#51 Time-Waster: An unproductive office layout

You need the sales file to keep up with your collections. You need the computer file to keep up with the cost-accounting information. You need the file for new products to help the salespeople in the field. You spend a great deal of time walking to the files because the file is not near your desk.

Solution: Make a list of the information you need during a normal day. Is the information available to you? Where is it located? Why not move the file closer to you or your office. Look at the office layout on Illustration #4A. What about the other people in your office? Do they have important information close to them? Make arrangements to move the information as

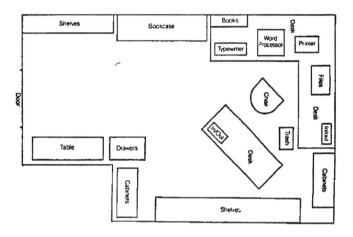

Figure 6

close to them as possible so they can save time and be more productive.

#52 Time-Waster: Letting the clock dictate your schedule

You have a great deal of work and too little time. You try to finish it within the normal 8:00 A.M. to 5:00 P.M. schedule. Your deadlines are increasing, and you find yourself falling further and further behind.

Solution: Try to start earlier in the day. By starting at 7:00 A.M. each day, you increase your weekly work schedule by five hours, without listening to your phone. Many time managers find that after five o'clock, when the office empties, a quiet and productive atmosphere appears. You manage your time and activities, not the clock on the wall.

#53 Time-Waster: Rechecking everything

You redo everything. The list for the Christmas party is checked, added, subtracted, redone over and over again. You redo the internal report on telephone use seventeen times because you don't want to be associated with anything that isn't letter perfect. You drive your people crazy with each minor mistake they make. You perfect everything. You make some changes even when changes are not warranted.

Solution: Ask yourself whether or not you need all of this stress-induced, time-consuming perfection. Do you need to recheck everything? In some cases it is essential that you strive for accuracy, but the perfection continues to spin and spin. Make a list of the time you spend checking things that do not need to be checked, and avoid them in the future. When you find your perfection activities are decreased, perhaps you can concentrate on other important activities.

#54 Time-Waster: Accepting excuses for poor time-management

The job was due at 2:00 P.M. today, Joe came into the office to explain, "My secretary lost your request for the job," and you accepted the excuse. This is the same excuse he used the week earlier. The people who make up the excuses lose valuable time, and you spend your time listening to them. Some of the most common excuses are:

> The auditor held us up on that report.
> I never received your call.
> The sales department lost the order.
> We didn't realize it was a top-priority.

Solution: You're in charge of the excuses that can be accepted. When you hear the same excuse used over and over—let the user know you will no longer accept it. Reject excuses and request action. Tell them you want performance not excuses.

#55 Time-Waster: Constantly reminding people that they lose or waste time

Timmy C. does too much typing, rather than permitting his secretary to do it for him. Sue spends time filing when she should be working on the word processor. Frank spends time talking about the local sports team when he should be scheduling production for tomorrow. When you see these workers acting like this, you should see dollars going up in smoke. You should see red ink on the profit and loss statement. You would like to go over to each one and tell them how they can better use their time. There is an easier solution.

Solution: No one wants to be told what to do. Everyone wants to feel he or she has freedom to do things his or her own way. Call a meeting periodically. Diplomatically tell them the importance of working smart as well as hard. Show them they can make their time count and get the rewards as well. Inspire others. Be willing to show them they count.

Be a good image for your people, not only by using your time well but also by showing people how to enjoy what they're doing. When you make work like play, you will get more work done. One manager from New Jersey, Allen P., invites his supervisors to a monthly meeting and hires a speaker to talk about time-management. He also gives them a free dinner. At the end of the meeting, Allan gives them a written summary in the form of articles and reports of the meeting. In this way, he reminds his workers of the importance of using time as effectively as possible.

Another time to remind people to use their time better would be when you go out to lunch with them. Get the individual alone and take the opportunity to remind him of his potential to use time better. Give him ideas of high-payoff work or work that can help him and your organization. Show him you care for him and the organization.

#56 Time-Waster: Making impossible demands on others

Your people are only human. They can accomplish only so much work. One sales manager from Dallas, Christine M., insisted that her salespeople wine and dine clients until the wee hours of the morning. Then she chastised them for not being alert and ready to go at 8:30 A.M. each day. These demands are impossible to carry out. The salespeople are "damned if they do and damned if they don't" and become confused and demoralized.

Solution: Be realistic in your expectations. When you require the impossible from others, expect results that are less than spectacular. People are appreciative when they find you willing to teach them how to do it. Successful time managers know you can catch more bees with honey than with vinegar, so be willing to let people do the best job possible and then let them know you're thankful to them. Be willing to assign them the small jobs, and then carefully give them positive reinforcement. Increase the demands with the carefully measured reinforcements until you reach your own level of success.

#57 Time-Waster: Not willing to face the truth

Bob V. knows that one of his employees has a problem with liquor. Betty I. continues to miss Monday after Monday and continues to complain of having a bad cold. Betty's work is continuing to suffer. She was one of the finest workers in the fabrication department; and now her work needs constant supervision. Her error rate is continuing to climb. Bob V. continues to put the problem out of his mind because he is not willing to face the truth: Betty's liquor problem is getting worse.

Finally, Bob V. calls Betty into his office. When Betty finally admits she had a drinking problem, Bob recommends AA, Alcohol Anonymous, and Betty is much improved. Bob V. also gave a toll free 800 number for anyone who needs help with alcohol; the number is 1-800-ALCOHOL. For people that might have a cocaine or drug related problem the 800 number is 1-800-COCAINE. Take the time to put your people first, and things second.

#58 Time-Waster: Failure to inform others of your whereabouts

There is nothing more embarrassing for your secretary or assistant when you're out of the office than to have a caller ask where you can be reached, and the secretary is forced to say he/she is not sure where you're located right now. This is especially embarrassing for you when the caller is your boss or an important customer who has something urgent to speak to you about.

Solution: Before you leave your office take the time to give your secretary or assistant the full information on your destination, including the full name, address and the telephone numbers of the party you will be seeing. If the number is changed or incorrect for some reason, the caller can get the right number with the name and address. If you plan on visiting two or more people, let your office know the approximate time you will be at the different places. Give the number where you can be reached at night for day messages, if you plan to be on the road all day. You will miss that important call if you fail to leave your number with your assistant. If you leave your whereabouts with your assistants, you will look more professional.

#59 Time-Waster: Lack of change for parking meters

You parked the automobile close to your destination. When you reach into your pocket to get some quarters for the meter, you only come up with a total of twenty-three cents.

Solution: Before you start your trip or selling activities, stop in your local store or bank and get sufficient change in quarters, dimes, or nickels. Once you have sufficient change, you can feed the meter without asking others for change. This will save you a great deal of time.

#60 Time-Waster: Not setting a value on your time

People ask your opinion on the solution to one of their problems. You like to help others and want others to think highly of you—so you're willing to offer this information quickly and accurately. You gain a reputation as someone who gives information away for nothing.

Solution: Put a value on your time. One consultant from Miami, Murray C., did a great deal of work for small-business people to help them set up marketing and management plans for their organizations. When Murray C found he was spending a great deal of time without billing any of this time out to his clients, he decided to set a value on his own time. He decided to charge $50 an hour to pay for his very valuable time conferring with small-business people. Murray found that his volume increased when he increased the cost of his time. Most of his customers understand Murray's need to be adequately paid for his services.

#61 Time-Waster: Line Cutters

You're waiting to get the tickets for your trip to New York.

It's a busy time at the airport. You look down at your watch and when you look up a tall man is standing before you. He was not there earlier. He simply cut into your line and tied to steal some of your time. Do you look the other way and say nothing, or do you tell him you have a right to your rightful position?

Solution: Why let others take your place in line? If you permit this once, it's easier to permit it again in the future. Be diplomatic and assertive to let him know that your position is important to you. Try this:

You: Sorry, but the line forms at the rear. I have waited twenty-five minutes to reach this position.

Line Cutter: Oh, excuse me, but I was here right along.

You: Sorry, but that blonde woman has been in front of me for the last twenty-five minutes.

Line Cutter: Oh, all right, I will move.

#62 Time-Waster: Lack of feedback

You assign the difficult personnel assignment to Greg P. and tell him to keep you posted on his progress. Your boss wants the job finished by Friday. Late Thursday afternoon, Greg is forced to go home with a bad case of the flu. You must now explain to your boss why you need additional days to finish the job. As you review the case in your mind, you ask yourself why Greg did not let you know earlier that Friday's deadline was impossible to keep. You need more feedback to manage properly. Let's see how you can attain it.

Solution: Force your assistant, in this case Greg P., into giving you feedback on the progress of the assignment. For example, you can get the valuable feedback by using the following tactics:

Greg, you will be attending the Clark meeting on Monday; let me know then how the assignment is going.
Greg, please let me know the status of this assignment. Even if you're on time, please let me know Monday. All right?
Greg, I cannot just assume that things are going all right. Let me know how things are going.

#63 Time-Waster: Leaving current projects or assignments back at your office or home

Solution: Try to keep things in your pockets, attache case, glove compartment or purse so that you can work on these jobs when you get spare time. One time manager, Tracy V., finds that much spare time can be found while waiting for the meeting to start, waiting at the dentist's office, waiting for the mechanic to fix her automobile, or commuting to and from work. Use this valuable in-between time to your advantage.

#64 Time-Waster: Delaying specific appointments

Solution: You know that you must meet with Lee M. to set up the next speaking program for the fall. While you're speaking to her on the phone, make specific appointments right then and there to avoid another phone call later.

#65 Time-Waster: Excessive clock watching

Solution: Nothing upsets a relationship with an important person, or customer as much as your excessive searching for the correct time from the clock on the wall or your watch on your wrist. By referring to the watch, you're really telling your visitor that time is fleeing and that you must move on to other things your visitor may feel are even more important than he.

Focus instead on the task at hand—the report you write, the model airplane you built, the good conversation on the phone— then time almost ceases to exist. You will communicate with others based on the way you handle your time. If you seem nervous and always watching your watch, you will make others nervous around you.

#66 Time-Waster: Avoiding the important little things

Solution: Good time-management means to stress the little things that give you a handle on your job. The little things like getting notes to your assistants about current projects may seem small, but the total value adds up to your ultimate success. Do the small things that are necessary in your job. Take Ed M. from Montana. He is a very successful college instructor because he takes the time to do the necessary things to stay on top of his job. For example, Ed assigns the homework early, collects it on time, and gives the future assignments on time to permit his students the necessary time they need to finish them. Ed gives the impression that he means business and uses his time well, serving as a model to his students.

#67 Time-Waster: Involving everyone on one project

You want the advertising campaign completed for your customer on time. In order to do this, you involve too many people in your office to work on the campaign. People get into each other's way, and instead of saving time and effort, you lose it. The final result is far from the best work possible. Your customer is upset and so are you.

Solution: Put the most capable people on the job. Decide who is the most capable, interested, and motivated to do the work. Choose quality rather quantity. Once you delegate the job, get out of their way and let them do it.

#68 Time-Waster: Too many personal and outside activities

You're getting ready for an 11:00 A.M. meeting with the most important depositor of your bank. The phone rings, and on the other end of the line is your rabbi asking you about the Temple's fund-raising project for next Tuesday night. You quickly affirm your availability to the rabbi, but he then tells you about the latest changes in the temple, their future goals, and on and on. The sweat begins to pour from your forehead, and you take a quick look at the clock to find that in five minutes your important meeting will begin. You tell the rabbi you must get off the phone. As soon as you put the phone on the hook, it rings again. The coach of the women's field hockey team wants you to coordinate the season's ticket advertising campaign to increase their funds. Your personal and outside activities are putting a stranglehold on your career goals.

Solution: Take a hard look at all your personal and outside activities. Why did you start each one? Did it change over time? Is it necessary today? Carve away the outside activities that are non-essential and keep the activities that are important to you.

One manager from Kansas tries to restrict her personal or outside activities to after working hours, After 6:00 P.M. She will take calls or talk about her outside activities.

Another politician from Massachusetts was beaten for his bid for governor of the state. In-between election periods, he decided to take a job in a Boston law firm. While at the law firm, he made a policy not to accept calls or activities for his personal or outside activities while on his job. Cut the excessive outside activities to a minimum.

#69 Time-Waster: Letting unimportant things become important to you

You spend fifteen minutes on the preparation for your meeting with the personnel manager concerning the need for more clerical help in the Easton plant. Sue V., your assistant, asks you about the location of your office supplies. She ran out of white paper. Fred V., another assistant, wants to know why the Easton plant sent the 600V report on fixed assets. He is really trying to satisfy his own curiosity.

Solution: Do not fall into the trap of giving attention to unimportant work. Don't permit the unimportant things to pull away from your #1 priorities. Continue to go back to the important work. Put a value on your time. Do you want to spend one hour to solve a problem worth only $10? Your time is worth a great deal more than $10. Let other people know that you value your own time. Do not stand to have other people pull you away from the high-payoff work. Force others to take on their own duties, so you will be free to pursue your important jobs and projects.

#70 Time-Waster: Using the "When I get time, I'll do it..."

Many people rationalize their lack of ability to get things done by saying that when they get time they will be able to do it. It almost assumes that time can be put into a bottle and used when needed. When you get time, you will write the novel, paint the backstairs, take your family to the art museum, learn to ski, take your feeble uncle out to lunch, start that new business, etc. Getting the time to do these things requires the ability to use the time you have right now. All of us get the same amount each day.

Solution: Make a list of the things you would like to do. In order to complete them, you must want to do them badly—so badly, you will think about them continually until you take action on them. You must move from the mental stage in which you simply think about the project, until you're so motivated you then take action on it. Successful completion of these projects means moving into the action stage. You move into the action stage a little at a time. Do the outline of the book first. Once that is complete, you can write the first chapter; then the second chapter, until you finish it. Use your existing time to finish those "When I get time..." projects, and feel better about yourself.

#71 Time-Waster: Yelling at others when the pressure builds up

You're trying to finish the presentation for your boss. Sue, your assistant, wants you to dictate that important letter to the main office. Fred, your assistant manager, wants an approval for the printing of your catalog brochure. To relieve the pressure, you begin to yell at Fred. Yelling at Fred will do nothing for the time-management needs. Your reaction to Fred is the result of the pressure building up around you.

Solution Choose the most important thing to do and start working on it. Good time-management requires strict discipline to implement the necessary things to make you a successful time manager. Break the jobs into manageable units, and do them one by one. Put the energy you would normally put into manageable units, and do them one by one. Put the energy you would normally put into complaining and yelling into starting it. Then work on putting each part together until you finish it.

#72 Time-Waster: Listening to only what you want to hear

Fred V of the accounting department asks to talk to you.

Once you accept to speak to him, you begin to tune out Fred's views. You view the accounting people in a particular manner: You begin to listen only to some of what Fred V has to say to you. Once you tune out, it is difficult to tune back in.

Solution: Stop what you are doing. Don't look down at your papers or do some filing when Fred V. begins to talk. Look directly at Fred, nod to him when you understand his statements, and be willing to stop him when he makes a statement you don't understand. Give Fred V. your undivided attention. When he is finished with his statements, be willing to summarize his request or statement to him. Once the summarization is made, give him an idea of when you can help him. Try not to promise things that are impossible to accomplish. Thank him for taking the time to talk to you. When people take the time to communicate with you, it means they care and trust you enough to share it with you. This communication is essential to getting informal and formal communications started in your organization. Proper listening gives you extra information and shows others around you that you care about them.

#73 Time-Waster: Mismatch of your activities and your desired goals

You made a commitment with your boss to do a profit analysis for your department before the end of the year. This profit analysis would play a key role in the effectiveness of the department. It may aid in a promotion to the manager of the department. Although you're aware of the importance of the goals, you continue to spend time on current activities that do not match the goal.

Solution: Visualize your successful completion of your goal in your mind. See the maintenance person putting up the sign on your door naming you to the manager's job. Think about the additional products and services you could buy with the increase in your salary. Once the visualizations are completed, put on your list of "Things to Do" the assignments you need to complete to reach your goals. Each day try to do something, no matter how small, to carve away at your important goal. Once you begin to do some small activities in the pursuit of your goal, it will begin to take shape. You will do more things to complete the goal.

THINGS TO DO TODAY! Date:_____

Urgent ✔

Done ✔

☐ 1.	☐
☐ 2.	☐
☐ 3.	☐
☐ 4.	☐
☐ 5.	☐
☐ 6.	☐
☐ 7.	☐
☐ 8.	☐
☐ 9.	☐
☐ 10.	☐

NOTES:

#74 Time-Waster: Lack of proper research before decisionmaking

Solution: Good time-management and proper decisions rest on adequate research into the subject matter. Take the necessary time to uncover the necessary information to make your decision. Take the example of deciding whether or not you want to take on this new client into your business. You should ask yourself the necessary questions. Do I have time to service this new client? Do I have adequate information about the potential client to make a decision about accepting him as a client? Why did he want to hire me in the first place? What relationship, pro or con, did he have with his previous consultant? How much background investigation of the client is necessary? Take the research and determine the best possible answer to your question. If you have too much information or research, use only the relevant information to make your decision.

#75 Time-Waster: Not evaluating the people around you

Solution: How helpful are the people around you? Do they help you reach your goals? How can each person be more efficient? Do they work harder or smarter. A good time manager must strive to make the people around him/her work smarter, not necessarily harder. Research in the motivation area found that the yearly meeting between work and supervisor to review the worker's performance is one of the most important meetings in the year. At this meeting you must grade the worker's performance and set goals and objectives for the next year. By letting people know what you expect of them informs them that you're organized. As a supervisor or manager, you hold a very important position in their lives: you're the model, the time-management model, the human relations model, the management model. Take the time to evaluate others. Remember to empathize both the positive and negative aspects. Too often, evaluations stress the negative, and fail to focus on the positive. Good time-management is evaluating others around you. You play the role of the director of the symphony, bringing into focus the prime talents and skills of others.

#76 Time-Waster: Failing to determine the reasons for your failure

The meeting with your clerical staff went very poorly. Your best customer sent you a very curt and nippy letter about the last shipment of leather. Your secretary is not talking to you. You send out letters without proof reading them first. What is the cause of these failures?

Solution: Stand back and analyze your failures. What went wrong? Is it the lack of interest you're showing to others? Is it the lack of attention to detail? Is it the problems in your personal life? Is it the procrastination on important things that hurt your chances for success? Go over the way you spend your day. Where do you spend the bulk of your time? Do you spend it helping others? Do you spend it doing routine paperwork? Do you spend your time trying to find important things to help you in your job? Do a time study to determine where you spend your time. (See Time Log.) Determine what other areas where you should be spending your time to reach success.

#77 Time-Waster: Thinking a time log takes too much time and effort

Solution: Successful people know where they spend their time. They have the ability to self-correct themselves into putting their time into the proper places. Take Elden V., for example. He's a life insurance agent for the largest insurer in the country. Up to six months ago, he was one of the largest sales producers in his office.

Illustration 8 Time Log

Date_____ Name_____

Time	Task	Priority Number	Comments on Effective Use of Time
9:00 - 9:15			
9:15 - 9:30			
9:30 - 9:45			
9:45 - 10:00			
10:00 - 10:15			
10:15 - 10:30			
10:30 - 10:45			
10:45 - 11:00			
11:00 - 11:15			
11:15 - 11:30			
11:30 - 11:45			
11:45 - 12:00			
12:00 - 12:15			
12:15 - 12:30			
12:30 - 12:45			
12:45 - 1:00			
1:00 - 1:15			
1:15 - 1:30			
1:30 - 1:45			
1:45 - 2:00			
2:00 - 2:15			
2:15 - 2:30			
2:30 - 2:45			
2:45 - 3:00			
3:00 - 3:15			
3:15 - 3:30			
3:30 - 3:45			
3:45 - 4:00			
4:00 - 4:15			
4:15 - 4:30			
4:30 - 4:45			
4:45 - 5:00			

General Review and Comments_____

Grade _____

During the last six months, Elden V didn't feel like working. He would go out of his way to read the paper, play golf, or do any other thing to slow down his selling. When he did a time log such as the one on page 70, Elden found it only took him three to five minutes to determine where he was spending his most precious, non-renewable time. When Elden found out the amount of time wasted, he changed things. Be willing to take the few minutes to do a time analysis on yourself to put yourself back into the productive use of your time.

#78 Time-Waster: Negative thinking habits

Solution: Your good habits are very important to your time-management. Good habits are using your assistant to help you reach the high-payoff jobs. Good habits are forcing yourself to start the difficult to start job. Good habits are saying "No" to your natural reaction of saying "Yes" to playing golf in the early afternoon, or staying too long on the coffee break, or wasting valuable prime time doing the non-essential things, permitting the important work to wait another day, week or month. Get into the habit of doing the things that will make you successful. Do the things that failures don't like to do. Make today the best day ever—even if it's not a high-cycle day. Force yourself into the habits that will make your time count.

#79 Time-Waster: Doing the job that is closest to you, or the one you're thinking about

Solution: It's easy to move from one job to another—to do the job you think about at that moment. All of us fall prey to doing the things close by or the jobs we're most familiar with. When someone asks us about that important goal you spoke about last week, we simply say we will start it tomorrow. We make up excuses, one after another, so we can kill as much time as possible. We hide behind the structure called "I don't have time to do it..." Do you have time to keep your job? Do you want to use your time better?

One young salesperson went to the library to determine where he should spend his time in order to make a success out of his job. After reading many statistics on salespeople, he found that the new salesperson must spend seventy-five percent of his time prospecting, or getting prospects for selling. Eight percent of your time should be spent preparing for your appointments, honing your skills, talents and knowledge of the material, so you can deliver the best possible presentation. The remaining time will be spent giving presentations directly in front of your customers. Your most important time will be spent when you close your prospect. You must take the time to permit the prospect to make his/her decision. Nothing happens until you get the signed order card. Move away from the temptation to do the job closest to you. Take the job that will give you the success you need.

#80 Time-Waster: Avoiding time-saving methods

Betty is the supervisor in charge of the computer equipment in her department. When she completed a time log, she found many hours are used to check service contracts, service invoices, and proof of service records. To cut down on this time, Betty developed her own "Down-Time Log" shown below.

Down-Time Log
Apple Company

Date	Equip.	Serial#	Time Started	Time Finished	Solution

This log was very popular, and the computer department is now using this log as well. A time-saving method can not only save you time but gain you a fine reputation as well.

#81 Time-Waster: Staying at your desk too long

Solution: Try to move away from that comfortable desk, where you have many papers, pet projects, photographs, and many other conversation pieces. Offer your meeting in the conference room. Or use the technique the former mayor of Boston uses. He holds a meeting and uses a coffee table. When the meeting is over, he collects the papers from the coffee table and goes back to his office. Another time manager, a famous advertising copywriter, stopped using his comfortable desk and purchased a much smaller desk, just large enough for his typewriter and a sheet of paper. With this lack of space to put little-used items on, he was able to get down to the work at hand, and became much more successful.

#82 Time-Waster: Looking up information, rather than setting up a system

You memorized a number of names of people in your organization, and their positions and departments. When you have the occasion to call them, you look their name up in the phone directory. You do the same thing at home when you want to call someone. You look them up in the phone directory or call directory assistance. The sands of time slide quickly to the bottom half of the hourglass.

Solution: Make a phone directory of the people you will contact in your organization. List the people who work in and out of your department. Why walk over to Sue's desk if you can make a quick phone call? One way to set up this directory is by listing people by their last names. Once you begin to use the directory, you will find it easier and easier to use. I used a directory on my first job and took this directory with me on the next job, and to the next job. This directory became my own personal listing of associates, former associates, contacts in specific fields. Use your phone directory to save time and energy.

#83 Time-Waster: Not considering your energy levels

Solution: Not only will the hands on the clock turn, but so will your energy cycle. Just as the hands on the clock turn from morning to night, your energy level moves from one level to another. For example, you may want to draw up a plan of your energy level such as the one below.

All of us, from the secretary to the supervisor to the corporate vice-president, are allotted the same amount of time: 8,760 hours a year. In order to get the maximum amount out of your time, you should consider your biological clock. Large warm-blooded animals in the tropics show two peaks of activity—late morning and late afternoon, with a lull from 1:00 P.M. to 3:00 P.M., the hottest part of the day—say Marcia J. Thompson, a social anthropologist, working at DePaul Hospital, and David W. Harsha, a physical anthropologist at the Louisiana State University School of Medicine. The summary of the study showed the following:

- Schedule your most demanding work for mid to late mornings.
- Move back your lunch hour to 1:00 P.M. or 2:00 P.M.
- Devote the early afternoon to less demanding tasks—solitary work.
- Return to more vigorous activity in late afternoon. Don't waste these hours cleaning up earlier work.

#84 Time-Waster: Lack of understanding of your actual and potential activities

Solution: Take the time to look carefully at the numerous actual and potential activities such as:

Training assistants	Attending Time-Management Seminar
Talking on the phone	Shopping
Handling correspondence	Playing Golf
Taking a college computer course	Reading and interpreting reports
Handling difficult situations	Writing new policies for accounting department.
Taking lunch and coffee breaks	

This list just scratches the surface. Make you own list in the space provided below. Focus on the activities that are important to you, delay the unimportant, delegate the activities.

List of actual and potential activities

Time	Energy Level
8:00 A.M. to noon	Low Level
Noon to 6:00 P.M.	High Level
6:00 P.M. to 9:00 P.M.	Alert Level
9:00 P.M. to midnight	Fairly Alert
Midnight...on	Resting

Now that you have done your own plan, focus on how to best construct our day to best utilize your day. For example, in the rough plan above, you would avoid important meetings and activities during your low-energy period and set up important meetings during your high-level-energy periods. In short, focus on the highs and tolerate your lows. An example of this is how you can use 100 pounds of steel. If you molded your steel into horseshoes, you could make $125 from the steel. If you used the steel to make razor blades, you would make $225. If on the other hand, you produced balance springs for watches out of the steel, you could make $250,000. In coordinating your energy-level periods, you could maximize the total amount of your time and reap the highest rewards. Good time-management means to determine the best possible way to use those precious minutes and hours of time each day.

#85 Time-Waster: Not hiring out services to others

You may be the type of person who wants to do everything by yourself. This behavior carried over to situations at home as well. One good example is the salesperson who earns $25 per hour while selling and finds that he wants to paint his own house during working hours. Instead of hiring someone to paint the house, he wants to hire himself, an amateur, to do it. Why not hire someone with experience to paint it.

Solution: Before taking on jobs you're not interested in or feel you're not qualified to handle yourself, choose someone to perform the services for you. Take the example of Bill K., a manager of training for a large steel company. He found himself getting behind in his management workshops when one trainer quit and another had a heart attack. Bill K. considered doing the workshop himself until he looked at the in-box on his desk. He started thinking about the high-payoff he had promised his boss. Once Bill K. gave enough to his work, he decided to hire a free-lance trainer to do the workshop until he had the opportunity to hire another trainer. Bill K. learned to become very selfish with his own time and demanded that the people who worked around him perform their own jobs thoroughly. Be willing to hire the necessary services to help you manage better.

#86 Time-Waster: Failing to confirm your appointments

You're meeting a customer on the road, and want to be sure that the time and the place are correct. Since you made the appointment three weeks ago, you want to avoid any misunder-standings or incorrect information. A salesperson from Massa-chusetts lost two hours in travel and waiting time because he did not confirm an appointment with the customer.

Solution: A day or two before your scheduled appointment, ask your secretary or assistant to call and confirm your appoint-ment for day, time, and place. Once the confirmation is made, you can prepare ourself mentally and physically for the appoint-ment.

#87 Time-Waster: Limiting yourself to doing one thing at a time

There is a standing joke about the politician who made it all the way to the presidency. This politician had trouble walking and chewing gum at the same time. Some jobs, like putting your department's budget together will require your full concentra-tion. Other jobs, such as driving your car to a customer's loca-tion, are opportunities to do other things, such as listening to your tape recorder or dictating memorandums to your secretary. Good time managers learn to do more than one thing at a time.

Solution: Be willing to add more and more activities at the same time as long as you do not hurt your performance. An accounting manager in Wyoming adds a column of figures on his calculator while waiting for someone to come to the phone. A salesperson from Ohio listens to sales management tapes in his auto between sales calls. A teacher in Missouri listens to classical music while he corrects homework assignments. A manager from New York has the ability to listen to his secretary while he looks for some materials he will need for the next meeting. Stretch your powers of doing more than one thing at a time to maximize your time-management.

#88 Time-Waster: Not using the multiplication factor

Solution: You're doing a job for your boss and you just assume it will have only one use. You finish the project and turn it over to your boss. Why not ask yourself about the other possible uses of this project or job? For example, a manager was writing a book on accounting. When he began the project, he visualized additional uses for the book, such as articles, tapes to instruct accounting, film on accounting, a radio show teaching accounting. Think about the other uses of your job, and you will save a great deal of time and effort. In the writing field, I know a number of writers who write a complete book before trying to sell it. In order to save a great deal of time and effort, many writers send a query letter, a letter describing their potential book. When the publisher shows a positive interest in the idea, the book can then be written or arranged contractually to be completed.

#89 Time-Waster: Your tasks or assignments are managing you rather than the reverse

You permit the various jobs to pin you down to your desk. The various jobs just pile up. You worry about how they will be done.

Solution: Put the most important jobs or tasks in one pile. The less important jobs can be delegated or delayed. Be willing to lessen your load of jobs by delegating once a day, preferably the same time, to your assistants or secretary. When you delegate on the same time each day, they will be looking forward to the work. Good time managers choose the most important job and get busy on it until it's finished. Do it now while you're thinking about it. Why keep moving it around on your desk? Take some action on it; do it now. You will feel more in control when you manage your activities. You're not forced into doing anything. Do what you want. Choose your activities. The best illustration of proper management of tasks in the experience of Christine V. of Montreal, a manager of cosmetic sales. Christine heard a speaker during a sales motivation meeting. When he was introduced, she heard he was making $400,000 a year using his time-management techniques. She called his office to set up an appointment to ask him about his time-management secrets. When she called his office, she was given an appointment in two months. She waited and then finally attended the meeting. When she asked him about the most important techniques he uses to earn such a high salary, he replied: "To do the most important, the most important activity at this time...."

#90 Time-Waster: Doing many things you did before you were promoted to your present job.

Solution: Look at your job description. Why did you get the job? Are you doing the things necessary to become successful in your present job? Do you fall back into the rut of doing the things such as excessive research, helping your assistant, doing many routine jobs while grooming yourself for the next step up the career ladder. Try to spend less time each day on the things you did in your former job. Carve out more and more time doing the high-payoff activities to do your present job.

Illustration #9

Time-Waster Check Sheet

Date	Time-Waster	Solution	Remarks

FOUR

Procrastination

"While we are postponing, life speeds by."
Author Unknown

Procrastination is a large word for putting things off until you're too late or forced to work quickly to meet a deadline, and the quality of your results suffer. You can procrastinate on your taxes, paying your bills, or meeting with an important friend or customer. When you procrastinating, life's important wealth—TIME—slips by. This chapter will focus on important time-waster situations to help you win the procrastination game and get the results you need.

#91 Time-Waster: Waiting for the last minute or deadline before you accomplish something

The best example of this time-waster is the millions of people who wait until April 14th or 15th to file their income

81

tax returns. Take the example of David S. of Massachusetts. In a rush to finish before the midnight deadline of April 15th, David S. rushed to the John F. Kennedy building in Boston. He was forced to get on his hands and knees to finish doing the return on the floor to beat the deadline. After wiping the sweat from his forehead, he completed the return just minutes before midnight. Deadlines can be prime time-wasters because we delay finishing the job earlier.

Solution: Focus on the rewards of finishing the job before the deadline. The one important benefit would be taking it right off the "Things To Do" list by completing it. Another benefit in the example of David S. given earlier would be the monetary rewards, being able to spend the refund on something important to him. In the case of the tax return, break the job down in different components and do each one. Spend five minutes on the job to get the forms together. Once you get all the forms together, add your total income; you will find yourself well started on the road to completing the job. Visualize yourself putting your feet up on the stool in your den with your hands behind the back of your head, feeling good about yourself, and finishing up a job or project earlier.

Once you start a job and get into the various aspects of it, you will find it easier to continue the job to completion. You will find that by accomplishing work on time, more and more good things will come your way, such as promotions, raises, and opportunities. By starting the project earlier, you will get extra time to order extra parts, get additional information, or whatever needs to be done. If the deadline is tomorrow and you wait until the last minute, those extra details, such as parts and extra information, will slow you down so you will miss the deadline. President Lyndon Johnson made a very important remark about his career and time-management: "The harder I work, the luckier I get." By putting the work out each day, LBJ found that eventually it paid off for him.

#92 Time-Waster: Under-estimating how long some job, errand, or trip will take

Scott G. is a young attorney working hard to build his career. He recently opened a new office and hired one secretary to work with him. He spends the morning in court, and he has appointments in the afternoon. One afternoon recently, he looked at his watch at 3:50 P.M. He remembered that he had to renew his driver's license at the registry. This was the last day to do it. He left abruptly to complete this obligation. When he arrived at the registry, there was a large line. He spent an hour in line.

Solution: Scott G. should consider delegating this job to his secretary. Perhaps he could accomplish this job on his lunch hour to keep his prime time for his new appointments in the afternoon. His time is too valuable for running errands or doing clerical jobs. Be willing to give yourself extra time to drive to your destination. A real time-waster is trying to make up for time by speeding on the highway. One salesperson from Minnesota drives to the customer's city, stays the night, and then prepares for the appointment. Give yourself the necessary time you need to finish a job.

#93 Time-Waster: Hiding jobs or problems under your desk cover or other places

You're faced with a problem. You cannot solve it. It is new and you have never dealt with it before. To get it out of your sight and mind, you slide it under your desk cover. No one will see it there, especially me; perhaps it will go away.

Solution   Unpack those hidden jobs from your desk cover; you cannot finish them beneath that cover. Take out one of those difficult jobs each day and put it on your "Things To Do" list.

Once you start to work on it, you will be on your way to finishing it. If you run into a problem and cannot finish the job, ask for some help. Oftentimes by going to the right person, you can get enough answers to move back to the job and finish it. You cannot take the chance of leaving the problems under your desk cover, because when you go on vacation, or away from your job for a few days, someone will find them. This is best summed up by Aristotle's successor Theophrastus, who once said, "Time is the most valuable thing a man can spend," so use your time on those difficult jobs you try to hide.

#94 Time-Waster: Spending too much time sleeping

If you spend eight hours each day sleeping out of the total twenty-four hours given to you, that means one-third of your life is spent sleeping. If you live to be seventy-two years old, a total of twenty-four years will be spent sleeping. Although each person varies in the amount of sleep required, it would be well worth looking into a possible re-evaluation of your sleep time.

Solution: Get up one hour earlier and spend this time any way you like. It might be used to plan your day to do something in your professional goal area or to do something in your personal goal area.

Another solution to cut down on the amount of sleep is to try to stay up an hour longer each evening. During that hour you could attempt some short term goals, some professional or lifetime goals. Some time managers stay awake by listening to an all night or late night radio show. Others exercise to keep their bodies alert to carry on with extra work into the late hours of the night. Take the steps necessary to cut down on the amount of time you sleep.

#95 Time-Waster: Delaying a job or assignment because you're afraid to make a mistake

Solution: All of us want to do everything or almost everything right without making a mistake. Unfortunately, to accomplish anything requires that you take a risk. In some cases, it means making a mistake or two. Good time managers realize that a mistake or two will happen. It will be up to you to learn from your mistakes and avoid them in the future.

As your self-confidence grows, so will your ability to accept mistakes. Although you man not be proud of your mistakes, accept the fact that they are the by-product of your efforts. Without the mistakes, you would never make the progress you need. Take your mistakes, and learn from them. Make a list of the mistakes you have been making. Include in the list the strategy you can take to avoid the mistakes in the future. Cut the mistakes to a minimum; but remember, when you stop all mistakes, you probably are being too conservative and not attempting too many things.

#96 Time-Waster: Delaying making a call or appointment to that important person

You want to see Dottie Clark to explain something to you about the medical payment plan. You hope you will see her in the hall to ask her about it. Or perhaps you will find her in her office alone to ask her. Time slips by and you never get the answer. Your wife continues to ask you about it. You use one excuse after another. It begins to drive you crazy.

Or take the example of Sue Thomas, a sales representative for a travel company. She finds that her potential customers will only buy from her when the timing is just right. If she tries to sell to them during their busy time of day, the customer will lose interest or in some cases even terminate the sales presentation.

Solution: Timing can be a very important factor in effective time-management. The best approach is to call Dottie Clark and set up an official appointment, rather than hope you will be able to talk with her in the hall. Prepare for the appointment by bringing a list of your questions so you don't waste your time or Dottie's.

In selling, an important key to success is making calls. The more calls you make, the easier it will be for you to get your share of the sales. An excellent time to reach one potential customer may be the worst time to reach another in a different field. Try to avoid calling on potential customers during their busy time of day. For example, you would not call on the owner or manager of a restaurant during lunch time. Try to set up a schedule indicating the best time to reach each prospect. These can be noted in individual account records for easy reference.

#97 Time-Waster: Delaying a job until a crisis results

Joe V. knows he needs a new production machine, but since business is off a little this summer, he decides to wait until the fall to make the purchase. Bill S., the maintenance manager, knows he should have a maintenance folder for each piece of road equipment, but he delays his paperwork because he has 100 other things to do. Both situations are procrastination plans at work, and will continue to work until the crisis results.

Solution: Visualize that crisis falling right into your lap. You're embarrassed. You tell yourself you should have acted sooner. Avoid the excuses, the wasted time of explaining why you failed to act, or the rationalizations of your actions. Act now!

For Joe V. the crisis will occur when the salesperson or the production machine tells him that if he does not buy the new production machine within thirty days, the price will go up by seven percent. Since the production machine costs $250,000, that will be $17,500.

For Bill Sullivan, the insurance agent requested a formal maintenance record program. To comply with federal regulations and watch insurance claims, Bill S. found the time to do it. Less than a year later, one truck driver had a very serious accident in New York. All the maintenance records were required in the case, and fortunately Bill S. had the records available. Don't procrastinate, waiting for a crisis, because it will finally arrive.

#98 Time-Waster: Avoiding asking about a better idea or ways to do something

You try to do a particular job, but find you cannot finish it. You have an idea there is a better and faster way to do it. You have a choice of continuing to work on it, or asking someone who knows something about it.

Solution: There are some situations in which you need help from others. Why spin your wheels when you might be able to get some direction or answers to finish your job? It might mean asking an associate at work, or it might mean asking someone with special knowledge about a particular area. A good time manager knows how to tap the knowledge of others around him and is willing draw people out. One time manager from Delaware asked his boss about production. His boss turned to him and said, "Have you read the three speeches I recently made on production?" This was just the information he needed to do his job better. Be willing to ask the right question to save your time and effort.

#99 Time-Waster: Storing important papers in various locations

Your attorney will ask for a copy of one of your important papers, like your divorce papers, or your birth certificate. You spend a great deal of time trying to find them. You lose time and energy. There is a better way.

Solution: Keep all your important papers such as your divorce papers, marriage certificate, military papers, adoption papers, birth certificates, deeds in your safe deposit box. You might be able to rent one at your local bank. This is an important time-saver for you.

#100 Time-Waster: Waiting for the right time or waiting until someone comes to your rescue on a job

Solution: Try the five to ten minute plan. Simply commit five or ten minutes to the project. By spending such a short term period on the project, it will break the inertia, and you can continue on. Some writers find themselves in the procrastinate web. They sit down in front of their typewriters and simply start writing for five or ten minutes to break up the procrastination spell. Once the writers write a half page or a page of copy, they have confidence to go on. Procrastination is a mixture of factors. One important element is confidence; and once you lose confidence, the easier it will be for the procrastination problem to grow. Develop an image of yourself as a doer. See yourself getting the important work done.

Take Nancy for example. On Friday she has a report due for her boss on scheduling of seminars for her company. Nancy procrastinated until the day before the report is due. Her excuse is to wait until the right time, secretly hoping someone else would do it for her. When Friday arrives and she does not deliver the report, she is forced to tell her boss she needed more time. Let's listen to the conversation:

Nancy:	Sorry, Sally, but I cannot give you the report today. I will work all weekend to get it ready by Monday.
Sally:	Monday is fine, Nancy, but I asked you in plenty of time. What seems to be the matter?
Nancy:	Oh, the typist took too long and the Able Company sent me the wrong information. I'm so sorry.
Sally:	Don't be sorry. Be mad at yourself for waiting until the last minute. Managers must manage themselves. Successful managers find procrastination common to everyone. There are a lot of unpleasant things in life that must be done just the same.
Nancy:	Are you trying to say that I should be harder on myself and the people working for me? I want to do a good job and be liked.
Sally:	Yes. I hired you to be a manager, not a worker. Push the people around you to get their best work out on time. When you develop a reputation for tackling the unpleasant tasks, the more these tasks become routine and less bothersome to you.
Nancy:	Thanks for your ideas. I plan to use them in the future.
Sally:	Making an effort is the most important decision you can make for yourself.

Be willing to make an attempt to curb your procrastination. It takes doing a little at a time, but it can be done successfully.

#101 Time-Waster: Blaming others for your procrastination

Solution: You're really getting back at your boss by procrastination. As you procrastinate, the pile of work becomes higher and higher. You get further and further diverted from doing productive things and get behind on everything.

Put the blame where it belongs—right on your shoulders. You're the one who can change into a productive individual who will gain a reputation for being a doer. Once people think of you as a doer, combined with your own confidence of being a doer, you will spend time in productive work.

#102 Time-Waster: Not using today to prepare for tomorrow

Solution: Just as the farmer works hard during the full growing season to get his crops in the right condition to maximize his harvest in the fall, the same applies to your time-management style. Get the high-payoff work done, then you can choose a reward that is meaningful for you. Visualize the reward to motivate yourself to do your important jobs. Take special advantage of the slow periods of your business or job to get the work done. A good example of this concept is the following fable:

> ...Presently up came a grasshopper and begged the ants to spare her a few grains, "For," she said, "I'm simply starving." The ants stopped work for a moment though this was against their principles. "May we ask," said they, "what you were doing with yourself all last summer? Why didn't you collect a store of food for the winter?" "The fact is," replied the grasshopper, "I was so busy singing that I hadn't the time."
>
> —From Aesop's "The Grasshopper and the Ants"

#103 Time-Waster: Trying to work with excessive noise, confusion and turmoil

Much procrastination is the result of people trying to accomplish their work in the environment of turmoil. This might be at home, in the office, or in the plant. You must take steps to close the door and leave outside your unhelpful elements. A good example of this is a very successful author who when he gets a good idea for a book, simply closes the door to his den and stays in that room until the book is completed. He has his food sent into him, and the bathroom and bed are in the same room. He stays in that room until the 1,000-page book is complete.

Solution: You may not be able to accomplish a task like this author, but you can take some measures to get the privacy you need to accomplish your tasks. One young mother who went back to college found that in order to keep up with her reading she had to post a sign on her bedroom. The sign said she would not be available from 3:00 P.M. to 5:00 P.M. each day. The children and her husband have adjusted to her needs. Things are going smoothly at home, and the young mother is getting a B grade in a marketing course.

#104 Time-Waster: Personal talk

Solution: You want to finish that sales report by tomorrow for your boss. You keep returning to Stan's office to talk about the ball game, your financial problems, or your problems with your children. Personal talk is important to develop and maintain friendships, but excessive personal talk keeps both you and your friend from getting important work done. Save your personal talk for lunch or during your break, or after working hours.

#105 Time-Waster: Procrastination on the important activities in your job

Solution: Get to know the essential activities to contribute to the success in your position. The accountant needs information to develop the accounting statement. The salesperson needs to make new customer appointments, and ask for the order to generate sales. The teacher needs all the effort possible to prepare the lessons for the next day. If you need to procrastinate, do it in the trivial and unimportant activities, but focus on the important ones.

#106 Time-Waster: You wait until late into the day to do the unpleasant job

You want to call your unhappy customer about the delay in shipping his order. You want to meet with Jim about transferring him to the evening shift, but you will call him later in the day. By late in the afternoon you're too involved in other priorities and projects and you procrastinate on these unpleasant duties. There is a better way.

Solution: Call your unhappy customer and Jim the first thing in the morning, and get these things out of the way. Once you finish your calls give yourself a reward like an extra cup of coffee or a new shirt or blouse.

#107 Time-Waster: You procrastinate because you look at the bleak, negative aspects of your job

You think about the problems, the reasons why things cannot be completed. You focus on why something cannot be done, why other people will slow it down, etc. You focus on the reasons why you cannot do your job, rather than getting right down to do it.

Solution: You must commit yourself to making the necessary change in your life. You are in control. Choose the people you feel will help you accomplish more, people who feel secure enough to help you accomplish your goals. Use the negative, bleak aspects of your job as information sources, so that you can set up a problem-solving situation. You can develop a plan, and then you simply work your plan until you finish it. Don't give in to the pessimist. Develop the strength to move on to complete the work.

#108 Time-Waster The perfectionist falls into the procrastination trap

Solution: Perfectionists want everything to be perfect before they attempt any job, and they also set some unrealistic standards for themselves. They delay starting the overdue project because of some negative or unfortunate result of some projects or assignments. I enjoy the quote that best sums up the need for persistence for this individual: "Winners lose more often than losers lose." Be willing to start a project even when you're unsure of the results. You will lose many times before you win. Be willing to admit that you are unsure of the final results, but you're willing to try the project anyway. Focus on the benefits that will result from the successful completion of the jobs. Take Fred F., a food technology manager with the government. One of his jobs is to give case report results within forty-eight hours of receiving them. With little time and a full workload, Fred finds it nearly impossible to give case reports within this time frame. Fred needed a better system, or he will spend all his time giving excuses for not meeting the forty-eight-hour timetable. By giving numerous excuses and complaining about his lack of help, Fred is procrastinating and not using his time to the maximum. After spending some time in a time-management seminar, he discussed setting up a #1 priority. Fred established his #1 priority to set up a system to give these case reports. Fred determined that a new system for handling the case reports was high-priority and it was urgent to be completed. He was able to handle the procrastination problem.

#109 Time-Waster: You procrastinate because you pamper other people

You correct Betty's mistakes and miscalculations rather than giving them back to Betty to correct herself. You continue to write up the investment bid proposals rather than show Christine the proper way to do this assignment. You do the research for Chuck, even when it requires you to stay late.

Solution: As long as you develop a reputation for doing the work for others, you will find your in-box filled with uncompleted and poorly prepared work. Who is working for whom? Pass back the shoddy work to the individual who did it.

Training is essential for all the people around you. You will be free to tackle the things you have avoided by understanding the reasons for your procrastination. Set up a system to handle the routine tasks, so you can get on with those special projects. Take the example of Terry V. of New Mexico. She is the food service manager of a large company; and when she first took over the position, many of the employees stopped her from doing her work by asking her one simple question after another. Terry knew they were pampered by their former boss, so she tolerated it for a few days then set up a plan of action. Terry called each of the employees into her office and told them to make decisions on their own level before taking it up with her. She also told them if they needed additional training for their jobs, she would set up some seminars with the training department of their company. The employees were a little shocked, but they liked the idea that Terry thought they could handle decisions on their own, and the idea they could get extra training to perfect their job skills, especially on company time and money. Terry showed them she cared about them and she meant business about sapping her time for too many questions. This plan of action worked. Terry is now the division manager, and many of her former employees are in supervisory positions because of their training and decision-making abilities. Be willing to force others to do their own work even when this means giving them additional training and some of your time in the beginning. Be willing to manage your time.

#110 Time-Waster: Procrastination caused by reverse delegation

You delegated the sales report presentation to Monica on Friday. It must be presented on Thursday of next week. Your work schedule is filled with the new plant opening in St. Louis, and you're trying to run the golf tournament at your club. Monica appears at your desk on Tuesday with the sales presentation half-completed, and she says, "Sorry, but I cannot do the sales presentation for you. I came down with a bad cold, and my mother is sick with it, too." Monica just presented you with the best example of reverse delegation available today. She is giving your work back to you. Monica puts the sales presentation folder on your desk.

Solution: Tell Monica you understand how she feels. The job is not an easy one, and it will require a great deal of work to get it done on time. Focus on the reasons why you selected her in the first place, and the benefits to her for completing this important assignment. Pick up the folder on the sales presentation and gently hand it back to her. Remind her about other successful projects she completed for the company in the past. Put the job (monkey) on her back, rather than take this on yourself. You will need persistence, diplomacy and tact to turn the reverse delegation into your favor; but it's essential to keep your sanity, and on the right track of the #1 priorities.

#111 Time-Waster: Failing to involve and reward others

You need the full effort from others to reach your goals and spur yourself on when difficulties set in. A reward can be monetary or it can be simply a kind word or a pat on the back.

Solution: Richard A. was assigned a project to bring in eight million dollars in receivables for his company. The cash flow was too slow and money was needed to pay expenses. Richard called a meeting of his collectors at the beginning the project and explained how the project would work, and how often he would review the progress, and how he would reward each person during and after the plan. When Richard was tempted to procrastinate on the plan, the other people working with him would talk about the plan, their progress, and success stories of others to move the plan on to full completion. By involving and rewarding others, the difficult plan will succeed.

Illustration #10

Time-Waster Check Sheet

Date	Time-Waster	Solution	Remarks

FIVE

Overmanaging Time–Waster Situations

Overmanaging is a major time-waster situation. While striving for excellence you fail to share the obligations and responsibilities with other capable people at work, home and play. Discover the specific overmanaging activities in your life and take the necessary steps to control them. A manager from Massachusetts suffered a serious heart attack because of his overmanaging activities. A business owner in New Jersey failed in her attempt to make her business grow during the last two years because of her concern to manage details and assignments of others.

#112 Time-Waster: Overmanaging employees

Sam X. is the owner of a small consumer goods manufacturing business in New York. He spend three hours of his precious daily time monitoring almost every move of this office employees. This practice makes his employees extremely nervous, saps their energy and self-confidence, and generates enough negative emotions to force people to quit. Sam X. spends a great deal of his time putting help wanted advertisements in the local paper and interviewing people for numerous positions because of his behavior. If we open the curtain on the reasons why this overmanaging is so predominate at work, we might find that it stems from lack of self-confidence, which breeds lack of confidence in others. Whatever the reason, overmanaging is a killer of time and money and must be stopped in its tracks.

Solution: You hired your employees to help you achieve your objectives. Why tie their hands and slow down their performance by checking them too often, getting into their day-to-day activities, thereby slowing everyone down.

Ask yourself this question: What is the most important thing I could be doing right this very minute? Is it helping my assistant? Is it checking the routine paperwork for accuracy? Or is it to bite into that #1 priority I promised myself or my boss two weeks ago? Where am I spending my time? Spend it where you will receive the high-payoff. Once you get so involved into your own projects, your employees will be free to get their own work done.

Successful time-management and self-management does not mean permitting your employees full reign; it means keeping reasonable control, checking on their progress within reasonable limits. Let people do their jobs, and take the time to reward them when they're done right.

#113 Time-Waster: An overmanaging boss

You want more responsibility, and to get this will require new jobs and assignments; but your boss keeps such firm controls over you, new experiences never see the light of day. You know the annual performance review is coming up in a few weeks, and important areas such as quality and quantity of work, reliability, and use of judgment would be considered in the review. You know that if your boss was not so much an overmanager, you could score very high on each issue. Let's now look at the way Sally V., an administrative clerk for a large insurance and advertising firm, handled her boss, Harold, during the annual evaluation.

Solution: Let your boss know you want the opportunity to stretch your abilities even more. The best time to make this point is during this very important review. Let's listen to the review.

Sally:	I'm glad you're satisfied with the quality of my work. I sure work hard to make the necessary results, and you supervise it closely and on a regular basis.
Harold:	Yes, but Sally, I try to keep on top of things. Our department is a very important one in this company. We want to keep up to the personnel department in performance.
Sally:	I understand, Harold, but I'm not sure I can accomplish a great deal more if I'm not permitted more freedom. I would like to learn more about the computer. I understand we bought some new software last week. I feel trapped doing the same billing week after week. I can do some detail media billing as well. I did this billing for my last company.
Harold:	You do an excellent job in the billing of clients. I need you there. I need you to teach Shelton how to bill our clients correctly.
Sally:	Yes, I will help, but I still want to branch out

more. I would like to become supervisor or manager one of these days. I feel myself falling into the routine trap, I want to make many more contributions. My work is accurate most of the time; it does not need to be rechecked so often.

Harold: I will keep this in mind. Thanks for bringing this to my attention.

Notice how Sally diplomatically but skillfully told her boss about the overmanaging and lack of opportunities to learn more to round out her experience and knowledge for her future career.

#114 Time-Waster: Over-reacting to the upsetting behavior of others

John K. embarrassed you in front of the other members of your department at lunch the other day. He asked you about a mistake that was made in your department that may upset an important customer of your company. You turned a little white in your face, but you bit your tongue and didn't say a word about it. When you went back to your office, you kept replaying the situation in the theatre of your mind, and this slowed you down all afternoon. You know you should not permit these small people, and even small things, to upset you and your performance, because time is time, and everyone gets only twenty-four hours each day.

Solution: When someone dares to say something to upset you, try to nip it at the bud, and answer the statement as promptly as possible. When the situation is over, forget it. In the army we had a saying: "Don't Sweat The Small Stuff." So we would not over-react to the things we could not control. A study conducted at the University of Nebraska by world-renowned cardiologist Robert Eliot reported two rules: Rule Number 1—Don't Sweat

The Small Stuff; Rule Number 2—It's all small stuff. And if you can't fight and you can't flee, flow.

You may never control every stressful or difficult situation that comes along, just put on the necessary equipment to arm yourself to your reaction to the upsetting situations. For some situations, it will require the placement of blinders on your eyes to avoid seeing each situation. It might also mean that you put on your football helmet to protect yourself from the jealous, uncontrollable people who feel you're a threat to them. Permit yourself to react as a rational, intelligent winner. Too often people react too quickly, too often, to situations that do not warrant it. Save yourself and your time by getting busy on other more important things. You will forget the trivial, irrational behavior of others.

#115 Time-Waster: Overmanaging in all areas of your life

You run things at work; you pick out work for others. You manage your husband's diet, recreational and exercise programs. You help your children with homework, schedule their social activities, and run your house like clockwork. You're tough on yourself, and you keep your house spotless. You wonder where the time is going. You want to accomplish some #1 priorities for yourself, but your energy level is low, and the hourglass is filling up. You wonder what you can do to salvage your time. Here are some ideas.

Solution: Look over your #1 priority or goal. Review your time as set forth on page 70 and of this book. Are you spending sufficient time to accomplish it? Everyone takes a vacation from a #1 priority, but excessive withdrawals from it means you're spending this time elsewhere, perhaps overmanaging others. Be selfish with your time. Concentrate on what is important to you. Why not take a small bite into the #1 priority today. Tomorrow take a larger bite. It simply means you will do a little more on your goal or priority. Draw back from trying to manage each and every bit of time of others. When your #1 priority looks more and more like a reality, you will feel more like finishing it.

#116 Time-Waster: Scheduling more and more in less and less time

You're overmanaging yourself. You fill your appointment book with too many appointments, you take on assignments with very short notice and deadlines, you're running later and later. You're also running out of excuses. You need more time to get things done correctly.

Solution: Pace yourself more. Try to plan your day on a more flexible and individual manner. If you're a morning person, plan to use more of this time. If on the other hand your best work is performed later in the day, gear your appointments and activities focusing on the latter part of the day. Take the example of Uni M. of Boston, who will space her appointments wider and wider in time when she finds her schedule too filled. Uni examines her schedule often to determine just where she is putting her most important resource, time, to work.

Looking at your schedule offers you a direction and a method to evaluate your progress. For example, did you finish the research by March 30th? Did you finish the manpower design by June 30th? If you're within the time frame, you can coast or get it done earlier. On the other hand, if you find yourself falling back, you might want to request some additional help to complete the project on time. By writing out the schedule, you will avoid the excessive worrying about finishing on time, and you can tell at a glance where you are in relation to finishing the assignment or goal. Your schedule will answer your questions for you. Use it.

#117 Time-Waster: Spending too much time with technical people

You worked for seven years in electronic testing for your company, then you moved into management, and now you find yourself as the supervisor of your department, along with the challenge of trying to do many other duties as well. You find yourself spending more and more time managing the testing department and are sadly neglecting your other duties.

Solution: Do you spend time in the testing department because you understand this department and feel confident about it? Ask yourself whether or not the time being spent in the testing department will bring you the payoffs you need. Are you a technical person? Or are you a more general type manager? You were hired into management to manage, not just one department or segment of the job, but to manage all aspects of your job. Become inquisitive. Read widely outside your main field of interest. Ask questions and gain knowledge outside your technical field. Open up to all aspects of your job. You will grow in your job, and your organization will benefit as well.

#118 Time-Waster: The perfectionist

You like to control things. You strongly believe that everything and everyone in your office has a duty to perform, all duties should be done correctly, and when things go wrong, or are left undone, you go to pieces. You show your feeling in a very immature manner. You yell, pound the desk, and even call names to let people know your true feelings. This behavior is upsetting for you and the people around you. People try to avoid you. They tiptoe around your desk, secretly hoping you will not recognize them. They act like you and your office are a huge keg of dynamite, and they want to avoid setting it off. This behavior is not helping your reputation as a manger or developing a rapport that will put you into the promotable ladder in your company.

Solution: Put your job into proper perspective. What do you want out of your job? What are the necessary things that must be done to reach your goals? What are the twenty percent of all the things you do that generates ninety percent of your achievements? If you can get those twenty percent items done correctly without expressing your emotions to the maximum, you will have energy to spare. Why blow up about the small, trivial, unimportant things that will only dampen your reputation instead of helping it?

#119 Time-Waster: Handling home problems at work

Fred S. is a single father. With three boys and two girls all under fourteen years old, he finds himself trying to run things at home from his desk at work. His daughter Sue had trouble in her social studies test and called Fred to talk it over in the middle of an important meeting at work. These repeated phone calls from home are primarily about things Fred cannot do anything about. A good example would be last week when Sue called during a busy day and said, "Greg hit me and hid my doll, and the dog won't eat."

Solution

Make a list of the types of calls you're willing to accept at work. The list may not only show emergency type calls, but also calls that you feel must be put through to you. Make an effort to spend the necessary time with your children during the evenings or on the weekends to prevent the excessive calls. The key here is to limit the routine calls, but to avoid making the requirements too stiff. What may be trivial or routine to you may not be so simple for your child. Communicate to your child on a regular basis and depend on your child to do his or her job well too. You want to develop confidence within your children. Consider the idea Charlie B. uses in order to keep up to date with what is going on at home. He invested in a beeper so his children can reach him in an emergency. You may want to consider this idea.

Illustration #11

Time-Waster Check Sheet

Date	Time-Waster	Solution	Remarks

SIX

Planning Ahead Time-Waster Situations

"Nothing is so dear and precious as time."
French Quote

To plan or not to plan. Too much planning takes time, but too little forces us to do more and accomplish less. How often do you look back on what you accomplished for the day, and wonder whether or not careful and more complete planning might help you complete even more.

Terry P. found that she was spending over eighty hours a week on her job, and still taking a great deal of work home on the weekend. Terry did an analysis of her time use and found she spent very little time planning how to do her work faster and quicker. She simply did one job after another.

Do you take the necessary time to evaluate other ways to do

107

your work? Planning is essential, because too many activities that consume your time cannot be changed anyway. For example, a major magazine did an analysis of how we spend our time, using years instead of hours and days. Here are the results.

Where do we spend our life time?

6 Years	—Eating
11 Years	—Working
8 Years	—Amusements
6 Years	—Walking
3 Years	—Reading
3 Years	—Conversation
24 Years	—Sleeping
3 1/2 Years	—Washing and Dressing
3 Years	—Education

These figures are only average statistics; some people will be higher in some categories, and lower in others. When we spend eleven solid years just working, and six solid years just eating, it is imperative to give time and energy to proper planning, so we can carve out some of the things we want in life. Planning means you must focus on daily planning, weekly planning, and life planning.

#120 Time-Waster: Avoiding your goals

A good time manager continues to pick away at his/her goal. He seems to make each minute count by always doing something to further the long-term goal. For example, what are the things you really enjoy doing? How would you like to change things? How could you change things for others? C. Clement Stone, one of the richest men in the world, now in his eighties, wants to change the world. His method is by helping people that need assistance to reach their goals. He is setting up scholarships to help poor people without the financial resources to meet their goals. It will be up to you to develop your own plans.

Solution: Make a list of the things you would like to accomplish in your personal life.   It might be a trip to Europe, living in a particular area of the country, building a particular house, returning to college, starting a new hobby, or finding new friends.

Personal Goals

Now determine what professional goals you would like to accomplish in your life. Would you like to become vice-president of the sales department, or run the printing department of your company, or start your own business? One of my clients, Julie H., wants to start her own mail order business specializing in imported Italian goods. She wants to combine her knowledge of Italian and her knitting hobby to develop the business. Fill in your professional goals below.

Professional Goals

Now determine what your short-term goals are for the next six months. What do you really want to accomplish during the next half-year? This short-term goal could be part of what you want to accomplish in your personal and professional goals. Choose the things that are personal to you. Do you want to set up a computer system for the ABC Company? Choose short-term goals that are meaningful to you, not to someone else, fit completely into your long-term goals, are attainable, and then be willing to work on them. Add a deadline for your goals, and the required action necessary to accomplish them.

Short Term Goals	Deadline	Required Action
i.e. Learn Computers	6 Months	Take Computer Courses at Business College

You will accomplish your goals if you list them on your daily "Things To Do Today" list. Just starting a goal is the first step in completing it. Keep on track and complete those goals to reach your objectives.

#121 Time-Waster: Dropping an important goal

Your chief goal is to become the manager of the accounting department of your company, but you drop it because your boss is young and the company is doing poorly financially. The goal just seems to difficult to reach. You want to write a book, but the book rejection letters are coming in faster and faster each day. You stop writing and drop the writing goal. You want to become an administrative assistant at your company, but your boss never gives you new experiences, new projects, new challenges to broaden and feed your ambition. Do you simply drop your goal?

Solution: Before you drop that goal, look at the benefits you will receive by attaining it. You could make more money, you could buy a new house, you could buy nice clothing, you could show others you can accomplish difficult goals.

Beth S., a secretary for an assistant manager of the department store wanted to become an administrative assistant to Mrs. Kessler, the top manager of the store. Beth became very discouraged because in her present job she found very little opportunity to learn new things and prepare for the administrative position. She wanted to drop the goal of becoming the administrative assistant. In order to keep that goal alive, Beth became friends with Laurie V., the current administrative assistant for

Mrs. Kessler. Beth began attending meetings for the staff, representing Mrs. Kessler in meetings with customers, accompanying her on business trips, attending supervision and management seminars, and working late some evenings to finish up important proposals. The more Beth learned about the job, the more excited she became about filling this job, or perhaps attaining a similar job with another company. Being interested and looking at the benefits of the goal rekindled the desire to attain this important goal. Keep this process in mind when you're tempted to drop a goal just because it seems slow-moving or difficult to reach. Remember the higher up the tree, the sweeter grows the berries.

#122 Time Waster: Taking a goal for granted

You just assume that by age thirty you will become the first manager of the computer department. You're interested, you work hard, and you secretly feel that this will be enough. You just expect success. You feel they owe it to you. The surprise of your life hits you when they hired someone else for the job. Let's look at the solution.

Solution: Learn what you must learn to gain the goal or the promotion. Sherri C. worked as a production worker at a local window company, until she decided she wanted to go back to college to finish her degree. When she finished college, she decided to go on to law school. She studied very hard and finished law school, but the next goal was to pass the bar exam to become a lawyer. Sherri knew that successfully passing the bar would require intensive studying sessions to cram all the law concepts and principles together. She scheduled more and more studying time for herself, cutting down her working time and socializing time to the minimum. Last month she received word that she passed the bar, and she will be a full-fledged attorney this spring.

Why assume you will somehow reach our goal? Never take

the goal for granted. Why do you just assume you will get the manager's job? You have to work your way to the position just like anyone else within the company. Successful people never assume anything; they just keep themselves busy working harder, learning harder, and trying harder than the person next to them. Whatever your goal, keep it in mind, visualize the successful completion of it, and do the most important thing right now to successfully reach it.

#123 Time-Waster: Loosely planned, lengthy meetings

You know what you want to cover in your meeting, but the topic gets off the track. You lose sight of the main objective. This includes the formal meetings that are called for full discussion of the new budget, or the informal discussions with employees who drop by to chat with you. These meetings move from being short discussions to long unproductive discussions that go nowhere.

Solution: In a formal meeting, make an agenda, listing the various points you want to cover in your meeting. Give the amount of minutes you will allow for each point if necessary. Stick closely to the subject of the meeting. Set a time limit for the complete meting if you feel your members like to extend meetings. Be willing to close the meeting when you get the answers to your questions or if your attempts to get the meeting back on the original track are unsuccessful. Be willing to terminate the informal meeting with the employee who stops at your desk. Use the following techniques:

Sue: Any party that doesn't get started by ten o'clock will be a dud. I gave a party for my girlfriend at Barket's Lounge. Some people said it was the best party they ever attended. Why, we had....

You: (Interrupting) Sue, sorry but I have a #1 priority to finish this report for a customer meeting this afternoon. Let's talk about the party at lunch sometime, or even call me at home tonight.

Sue: Oh, all right. I do have to get back to my office. See you later.

You: Right. See you later.

The formal meeting on the budget

Rita: We need the $10,000 for our department. Why did the shipping and receiving department get their increase last year? They get whatever they want around here. The supervisor is new, and so is their manager. I have worked here for twenty months now.

You: (Interrupting) Rita, let's stay on track. Please tell us why you want the additional $10,000 for your department. We are not discussing any other department right now.

Rita: Why? Well, all right. We requested the additional $10,000 to purchase a computer and a printer for the additional accounting required by the main office in Delaware.

You: Please pass forward our estimates for this equipment.

Be assertive. Let people know you have better things to do than listen to statements unrelated to the subject at hand. Most people understand that work will come before excessive personal conversations at work. Let them know where you stand, and you will get more accomplished.

#124 Time-Waster: Lack of a daily plan

You leave your home at seven in the morning for the twenty-minute drive to your company. As the sales manager of a large candy company, many thoughts fill your mind about the things that should be done to make your time count. You value time and want to use every bit of it. You know from past experience that once you start into your office, the interruptions, the meetings, the phones, the problems start and consume your whole day. You need a daily plan to survive.

Solution: In my interviews with successful time managers I found many of them using hours daily to set up their priorities for the day. One manager from Idaho, Fred K., planned for three hours a day. From the moment he awakes in the morning until the time he arrives at the front door of his company, he thinks about one priority versus another. Once he arrives at the company, he has a clear idea about what he wants to accomplish. Another manager of a large card and gift company, Donna L., does her planning during the evening, in the quiet comfort of her den at home. Donna finds that being far away from the office helps her to focus on the important things she wants to accomplish. Donna thinks about the plan and how she could accomplish it. She uses a daily plan format listed below.

Illustration #12   Daily Planning Wish List

Date	Priority Today	Completion Date
	1. i.e. Sales Quota for Dallas Store	Feb 10
	2.	
	3.	
	4.	

Now fill in the Daily Planning Wish List to guide you through your day. When you find yourself striving to do too many things, too fast, and find yourself spinning your wheels, go back to your Daily Planning Wish List and determine whether you're managing yourself, or just permitting people, projects, and things do it for you. Remember, you manage yourself. Plan your day, and work your plan.

#125 Time-Waster: Looking too far ahead of your goal

You know you want to finish that special project for your boss, but it will require assistance from Joyce T., the department head; it will mean spending time in the company library; and getting information from Rod C. in the accounting department. Your mind just keeps calculating all the things necessary to get the job completed. This advanced calculation in your mind causes more and more confusion.

Solution: Cross the bridge when you get there. Why worry about all the problems or situations until you reach them? Actress Goldie Hawn was recently asked about how she can combine a fast-paced career and her marriage and family. She replied, "I just do the next step in the plan I developed to reach my goal." Don't waste your time and energy worrying about all the things that could happen, or go wrong; just do the next important thing to finish your goal.

#126 Time-Waster: Setting limits on yourself

Sally W. worked in accounting her first year out of high school for a large electronics company in California. After only six months she was laid off because of a defense cutback. She liked accounting but could not find a job in this area, so she took a sales job for a rental company. She has worked in sales for four years now but would like to go back into accounting. Sally is afraid it would mean a salary cut, and she secretly wonders if she could really make it in accounting. Sally reads numerous classified ads for jobs available in accounting, and she would like to apply to one of those jobs. Sally's thinking patterns are beginning to put a stranglehold on her. Let's look at some ways to break this strangle hold, and embrace your potential.

Solution: Why limit yourself? There are too many other things in your life, including people, to trip you up, without your doing it yourself. If you don't know what you want to do, it will be much harder to do it. If you don't believe in yourself, it will be difficult to convince others. Come to terms with the facts of your own goals and ambitions, and convince yourself that you want to get ahead, too. Make a list of your skills, talents and abilities, and then match your special assets with your goals or ambitions. Try to look at your dreams as important and attainable, and put the energy and effort behind them. There will be days in which you feel in the doldrums, but it will be up to you to pull yourself up by focusing on your goal and working harder for it. There will be days when you face rejection, you lose an argument, or you make a stupid mistake and you feel badly about it. Don't take the rejection personally, but pick yourself up, dust yourself off and do your best, and look to the future with positive expectation.

#127 Time-Waster: Reaching for goals using old methods

Victoria R. is a sales representative for a cleaning supply company who wants to break her sales quarter record of last year by ten percent this quarter. Victoria tells all the other sales representatives, and even her customers, that time is money, but she totally ignores new ways to reach her goal. Many mangers want to succeed, but still try to use the same old tired methods and procedures.

Solution: Just like the heat that flows out of the house in winter when there are cracks in the foundation or around the doors and windows, goals are compromised when old methods are utilized to reach them.

Victoria wants to beat her last sales quota, but she will not use charge cards to save time or install a phone in her automobile to plan future appointments and check shipments for customers. Charge cards are records of her expenses for her expense reports and will save time getting receipts at restaurants and hotels. A car phone can add as much as thirty days to Victoria's business year, permitting her to communicate to her office, customers, suppliers, and others, while driving to a sales call. She can reschedule her day, and when she is away from the car, the phone will take and record her calls. Tighten up your methods and tools so you can reach your goals. The old methods might work sometimes, but you want to be competitive and be a winner, so use the best methods available to you. Organize your day, and your goal will take care of itself.

#128 Time-Waster: Too much planning, without action

Solution Take a look at the time you spend on your planning. Can you afford to spend this time, without action? Bill M. of Colorado is the legal counsel of a large business association who fell into the planning trap by spending too much time on planning instead of taking action. Bill decided that if he wanted to keep his job, he would have to change the way he functioned within the operation. He set up some deadlines for the court issues on taxation, hazardous waste, and unemployment benefits. Once the deadlines were set, it forced Bill to take the necessary action to meet them. Over-planning served as a way to procrastinate, to put off the important work by looking busy.

Examine the reason why you're over-planning, and then set up a situation to force yourself to put yourself into action. Look carefully at the benefits you will gain by doing your homework to get ready for that important meeting or presentation. Bill M. is now gaining a reputation for doing his homework better than any other attorney or lobbyist in Colorado. Do you lose valuable time by doing too much planning? Carve yourself away from the planning desk, and put yourself into the action desk to get your work done. Planning is important, but not as important as putting your energy, skills, talents and abilities to work.

#129 Time-Waster: Feeling guilty when your plan fails

Solution   *Winners lose more often than losers lose.* Winners know they cannot win every time. The law of averages works to split the wins from the losses. Why feel guilty about losing? If you stayed on the sidelines and avoided entry into the game, you would not feel guilty, because you didn't win or lose. Confidence is the result of achievement, and you cannot achieve unless you toss your top hat into the ring.

Instead of feeling guilty, put that important energy into a strategy for future success. What did you learn from this setback? How can you put this knowledge to work in the future. Turn those guilt feelings off by getting busy on your project or assignment.

#130 Time-Waster: Doing all the planning yourself

The busy executive, manager, business owner or supervisor knows he/she must plan, but taking all the planning on himself forces many other things to wait. Finally the day arrives when your total commitment to planning slows down the operation and puts your career growth into slow motion.

Solution: Visualize what your business will be like five years from now. What will your operation be like ten years from now? What can you do to make things easier on yourself, but make it better for your organization? Lynn L. is a very successful business owner in New Hampshire who recently leased a huge building for her booming lamp business. Lynn is very busy selling lamps at trade and craft shows and could not devote the time and effort necessary for planning. Lamps are difficult to sell, and Lynn had a special ability to sell them, especially at craft shows. She hired a consultant to help her do the necessary planning for her company. The consultant came up with many new plans including how to expand, how to hire more distributors, and how to produce more lamps to increase profitability. Lynn is now implementing these plans, and she is happy to see the company continue to double in sales year after year.

Another example is Tex C., the owner of a large tire recycling company who tried to do everything to build his business, including planning. In the beginning he was collecting tires from tire stores all over Texas. He did not separate the truck tires from the car tires, and just piled them higher and higher in a large storage yard. Now the truck tires are in demand, and because of the sheer volume of recycled tires, Tex cannot locate the truck tires. He failed to set up a plan to separate them in the beginning of the business. Tex C. told me he could make $100,000 a week if he had the truck tires separated correctly. Planning is so important, and so expensive if neglected.

Plan today for tomorrow's needs. If you cannot do it yourself, hire someone to do it for you. Put a system together to help you handle the demands of tomorrow. Don't wait for another day; today is the best day to do it.

#131 Time-Waster: Not paying attention to the cycle of your plan

Solution: Every plan has a cycle. In the beginning of the plan, you're optimistic and full of enthusiasm, and the process becomes a fast one. After the initial fast start, progress starts to slow down, and you're tempted to forget the plan, put it under the rug, and get busy with something else. A good example of this is a plan to lose weight. The first few days are successful, then it slows down. Don't fall into the temptation trap. Keep the plan going by throwing in some rewards. Keep charging ahead. Visualize how good you will look at the next party, how you can wear that new summer dress, how the new suit will look at the next sales presentation. Trick yourself into finishing your goal. A good crop at the farm goes through a cycle, from a seed, to a small vegetable, to medium and then a harvest-size vegetable. In order to reach the harvest, the crop must be watered, fertilized, weeded, and given the correct amount of sun. You must also do this with your plan. Keep charging ahead. Finish one stage, then go to the next one. Before you know it, the plan will take shape, and you will be on your way to finishing it. You're the captain of your ship. You can steer the ship in the direction of your goal. There will be storms, shipwrecks, wind storms, and problems along the way, but you must continue with your voyage. Let's look at how you can handle a real storm.

You decided to go on your boat alone. In the middle of the large lake you were happy because you cannot even see land. Out of a clear blue sky, the wind started to blow, a strong rain started to fall, the waves billowed up around your small boat, the lightening lit up the whole lake like a fireworks display, the thunder roared above you. The boat began to spin in circles, and you wrapped yourself around the mast and held on with all your might. Your stomach felt like a knot. Your biggest wish was to touch land again, hoping the storm would abate and move away. Your grip on the mast was weakening; you wondered if you could hold on. Somehow you gathered the necessary strength to barely do it. Finally the storm blew itself out, and the boat moved into calmer waters and another bright sunny day. All the work, stress and worry paid off for you. You fully enjoyed the calm, serene, beautiful lake as you moved back to land in the aftermath of this terrible storm.

This experience of battling a storm is similar to the daily battles with your goals. You must hold on and ride out the storm. There is a cycle to each goal, and you must stay with it to succeed. Keep charging ahead and taking the necessary action to move closer and closer to success.

#132 Time-Waster: Planning without prior research

Just because you plan does not mean you will succeed. Do you look at all the potential setbacks and problems that can result from this plan? How will the customers favor or dislike the idea? How will the other departments within your company react to your plan? How will the present situation in your plant or organization affect your plan?

Solution: One method of doing research is to ask questions of the very people you're planning to help. For example, if you plan a new product for your company, why not find out if your customers would be interested in buying it in the first place. You might want to ask what features they would look for in the product, what price they would be willing to pay, where they would purchase this product, what promotion campaign would be attractive to them. Get this valuable information and use it as the raw material to build your plan.

Bringing your plan to the customer first is essential to success in business. A well-known chef, Lucille M. of Boston, was surprised when a farmer from Vermont asked to talk to her in the kitchen of her restaurant. When she asked what he wanted, the farmer handed her a number of seed packages of various vegetables he planned on growing in the spring. Lucille selected some vegetables she felt would compliment the various entrees in her five star restaurant. This is an excellent way of saving valuable time by putting the proper research ahead of the planning stage. Find out what people want and then give it to them.

#133 Time-Waster: Delaying an employee training program

You know you cannot do all the work yourself. But the job keeps you so busy, you cannot take the time to train Janet V. to make sales over the phone; and Ben should be doing more sales accounting, but when can you train him properly. Rather than set up a plan to train them properly, you take more and more work yourself loading up your attache case to do it at home or on the train at night. You must make some changes or something is bound to break. You cannot take it any longer.

Solution: Many hands make light work. Happy employees will stay with your company. If you challenge your employees, they will appreciate it and make a greater effort for you. Carve out some time to plan for their training program. The time to train will be repaid by giving you more time to do the work you need to succeed in your job. Look at the training program guide given below to determine how you could set up a workable plan.

Training Program Guide

Name	Type of Training	Beginning Date	Ending Date	Inside/ Outside
Janet V.	Sales Training in Telemarketing	Feb 15	March 1	O
Ben C.	Sales Accounting	March 10	April 1	I

You are not forced to do the training yourself. In the schedule above, Janet V. was trained outside the office in the seminar at the local business college, and Ben C. was trained by the accounting manager at your organization. Once their training session is complete, write the trainees letters of congratulations and give them certificates of completion to show their training was important to you and the organization. Keep these employees going in the right direction to become lifelong learners. Plan ahead to keep your employees ahead in their fields.

#134 Time-Wasters: Lack of timely rest and relaxation

Solution: Hazy goals and plans produce hazy results. One of the reasons your results are not what you want is you're tired and cannot focus properly on your plan. Take your regular vacations, and see new attractions, new ideas, a different location each year. Vacations are essential to give you a new look at your plan, your job, your opportunities, and the full utilization of your talents. One successful time manager from Maryland takes four vacations each year, one week at a time. When he returns from the vacation he is refreshed and more than makes up for the cost of the vacation. Be willing to take the necessary time to keep your physical stamina high enough to reach your goals ahead of your competition.

#135 Time-Waster: Excessive complaining about why your plan isn't working

Solution: Use that energy in activities to make the plan work. Use that disappointment as a motivater. A top sales representative for a large car dealer in New Hampshire has days and weeks when he fails to reach his goal. Instead of falling into the habit of blaming the setback on others, he gets on the phone to call potential customers, he sends out over ten letters each day to prospects, and he continues to reread his goal and plan to achieve successful results. He learned that doing all the little things to make his customers happy, such as helping them with service after the sale is made and calling them back to remind them of the benefits of buying his car and the extended warranty helps him reach his goal. He also finds that staying close to the customer gives him a favorable opportunity to get recommendations to increase sales to family members, friends, business associates and others. Use the same techniques to maximize your time and your success.

Illustration #13

Time-Waster Check Sheet

Date	Time-Waster	Solution	Remarks

SEVEN

Orientation Towards Action Time–Waster Situations

"All my possessions for a moment of Time...."
Queen Elizabeth I

Achievers in life are not afraid to deal directly with the time-waster situations which slow them down from their objectives and projects. Achievers plan carefully, but when they feel a slowdown or reaching a plateau, they dig in more to produce the better work on time to beat their competition.

#136 Time-Waster: Poor filing system

Rich S. is a new sales administrator for a magazine publishing company, and receives many calls from clients and his sales representatives. He received two calls today during which he

125

could not find the client's files to discuss the subject intelligently. Rich files according to customer number, and by sales representatives.

Solution: Try an alphabetical filing system. Many time mangers find this system is the easiest system to use. Since your files are missing, you might consider requiring other people in your office to sign a "take out" sheet noting the name of the file removed from your office.

Review your system for filing regularly, and make the adjustments to meet your needs. Tell your secretary or assistant about your filing system, so they can use it when you're out of the office. When you take a file out of your office, sign the "take out" sheet.

#137 Time-Waster: Not using ideas from others

You're asked by the corporate office to come up with some new ideas for cutting the insurance costs in your plant. You know little about insurance; your background is in the engineering and quality control area. You must gather a great deal of information to get the plan to your corporate office by Friday.

Solution: Be willing to ask questions to answer the four W's: what, when, why, and where. It will mean doing research on the subject and tapping the resources of the people working for you or with you. Let's move closer and see how you can handle this situation:

You: Pat, do you have that information on insurance for me?

Pat: Here is some of the information on insurance premiums for our trucking operation.

You: Thanks, Pat. This will help.

Pat:	How is the project going?
You:	Good, but I need a great deal of additional information on life insurance premiums.
Pat:	I was under the impression Louise had that information. She works in that area.
You:	I haven't heard from her lately. (You turn away to the phone and dial). Let's see if she's in.

Notice how the successful time manger continues to ask questions and keeps moving in the direction of his project. He must keep the career vehicle in an orientation towards action. Be willing to ask the necessary questions to get the answers and information you need to succeed.

#138 Time-Waster: Interruptions

What are the interruptions? People? Machines? Routine jobs? Try to isolate the source of your interruptions. Once you find the source of your interruptions, you must try to do something about them. For example, George C., a business owner in Oklahoma, finds that his main source of interruptions is the negative thinking that forces him to use time he cannot afford to waste. He also reads a great deal of material that is unrelated to his job.

Solution   Run a check on your work production for a few days. What jobs are you finishing? Do you get the small jobs out? How do you handle the larger jobs? Do you delay larger jobs by permitting the interruptions to get you off the track? Good time managers know that doing a job is similar to staying on the road—you get side-tracked once in a while, but success results when you stay on the job.

Dan Rather, a top-notch news anchor for CBS, prepared himself for interruptions. On three pieces of paper he wrote the question: "Is what you're doing now helping the broadcast?" He put one copy in his billfold, one in his pocket, and one on his desk. Now when he falls into an interruption situation, he looks at one of those papers—it proves as a useful reminder. You can use this same technique. Try it!

#139 Time-Waster: Letting your fears control you

All of us have fears. The mortgage payment, the loans, the overdue bills can light the fire of fear within you. To permit the fire of fear to continue will slow you down to the minimum. Why think too far ahead? Stop, step back and think about what you want to do. There is more than one way to climb that mountain. Perhaps you can find a pass through the mountain. Perhaps you can tunnel underneath. Let's look at some solutions to the fire of fear.

Solution: Concentrate on the positive aspects of yourself, your job, your family, your hobbies, your talents, your abilities, anything that makes you happy you're you. Put your feet up on your desk and realize that you cannot lose the most important things to you—your wife, your husband, your children, or your abilities and talents. The worst thing you could lose is your job; and with the right desire, motivation, and enthusiasm you can get another job, perhaps even a better one. Remember the sun will come up tomorrow. No matter what happens, you must focus in on doing your best today. Lay your fears to rest.

#140 Time-Waster: Too many shopping trips

Solution: You shopped only for four days rather than for the full week. You must shop again in the middle of the week to replenish your supply. You put a few dollars worth of gasoline in your automobile rather than fill it up. You pick your two newspapers at different stores each evening after a long day at the office. Consolidate your trips, buy enough groceries to last at least a week or two, fill your automobile with gasoline on the weekend, and have your papers delivered to save you time and money.

#141 Time-Waster: Failure to save, use, and remember information

Solution: A successful consultant from Maryland uses a tape recorder to tape important meetings, record important summaries of meetings or telephone calls, play inspirational tapes while driving, and record ideas when they come up. Invest in a tape recorder to use all your important information.

#142 Time-Waster: Too many magazines

Your organization pays for your magazine subscriptions, and many magazines send you complimentary subscriptions. Your desk, table, and in-box is filled with magazines. Too much precious time is wasted keeping your magazines sorted, let alone reading them.

Solution: Examine each magazine. Does it offer new, relevant material to help you in your position? If not, cancel the subscription or transfer it to one of your associates or assistants. Susan F. of Minnesota, president of an advertising agency, delegates her magazine reading to her assistant, and requests copies of any articles of interest.

#143 Time-Waster: Excessive television viewing

Eileen E. is the owner of a home-based interior design business. She missed an urgent deadline for a large client because of her excessive television viewing habits. She watches one show after another.

Solution: Move your office away from the television. Tape important programs to view after you reach your deadlines. Limit your television viewing to the late evening. Reward yourself occasionally with free television time when you complete a special hard-to-complete project. Television in moderation can be relaxing and informative.

#144 Time-Waster: Too full, outdated files

Solution: Review your files monthly. When you find they are getting too full, thin them out by starting new ones. Perhaps you are trying to include too many items in one file. You lose time going through heavy files. When you change customers, products, services, or special projects, remove the files to give yourself more room.

#145 Time-Waster: Unused commuting time

You spend two hours a day commuting back and forth to work. That is ten hours a week, five hundred hours per year. This time is very valuable, and must be protected and utilized to the fullest.

Solution: Be willing to permit yourself to be creative in the way you spend this time. You can use your time in a variety of activities like rehearsing a speech, reading, dictating letters, listening to motivational speeches, an much, much more. You can squeeze a great deal more from your commuting time.

One management consultant from New York was dismayed by the great deal of wasted time by commuters on the railroad from New York City to Connecticut. Some people slept, others read newspapers, while others played cards, while still others simply did nothing. The consultant came up with an idea to use the time better. He set up a special car to offer courses in accounting, history, English, and math; and he awarded college credits for successful completion. The hours spend on the train were used to finish college or expand on a degree. The idea is so successful that many more railroad courses have been added, including graduate courses, to the college on the rails. Be willing to use your commuting time to your advantage.

#146 Time-Waster: Not demanding the finest quality of work

Joe V. is a good worker, but once in a while he has a tendency to turn out work that is less than desirable. You received some complaints from a very important customer about the quality. You don't want to lose Joe V. or your important customer. By not saying anything about the poor quality, you're sending a message that you really don't care about poor quality. If you let the poor quality pass this time, more poor quality will continue.

Solution: Talk to Joe V. about his work. Let him know that most of the time his work is good, but your business needs top-quality goods to gain a profit. Let him know how important his work is to the success of the company. Be willing to listen to his answer. Is there anything that you should know about the lack of quality in these products? Listen carefully to his response. Take the time to find out why the poor quality products are being produced. Once you find out why, then take the necessary action. Is it poor lighting in the factory, is it poor supervision, is it because of a poor inspection system, or a poor reward system for superior work? Take the time to find out the reason, and then take the necessary action to rectify it.

#147 Time-Waster: Trying to be an expert when you're not

Good time managers know that many projects or assignments are delayed endlessly or executed poorly because an expert is not involved, especially in the beginning.

Solution: Bring in the expert to get his/her knowledge to help you succeed. You might hire the expert for a limited time to get the job done. For example, a large computer company in Massachusetts found lagging sales, high costs, and high losses putting them behind their competitors. The founder hired a turnaround expert, someone who spent many years working with companies experiencing difficult times. The company is now working hard to reach success again.

#148 Time-Waster: Not charging enough for your time

Sue K., a young attorney, wanted to build her family law practice. She not only expanded her office hours at night and weekends, but was willing to talk over the phone extensively to her clients or potential clients.

Sue decided to take many difficult cases, some of which would take many months, even years to complete. Some clients called Sue to ask her the status of their cases, but other questions were often asked, and conversations that should have taken only a short time took ten to twenty minutes. Before long Sue found her work load getting larger and larger. She then made a check on her time usage and found that a large amount of her time was spent on the telephone. This was all unbillable time. To get ready to handle her numerous cases, Sue decided to take some action to save her time and practice.

Solution: Sue K. must let her callers know that she would like to speak to them, but it will take time away from working on their cases. Sue K. decided that she would charge her callers for taking her time. Let's listen to the conversation.

Sue: Hello, Sam, how are you today?

Sam: Fine, Sue. I called about the letter to ABC Company. When will we go to court?

Sue: I told you the last time you called. The letter went out June 1st. We will wait until July before we issue the warrant.

Sam: Sue, when can we expect some word on it? Where will we go to court? What has to be done?

Sue: Sam, we covered all of those questions last week. I have spent a great deal of time on the phone with this case. Spending time answering questions already answered solves little, and wastes a great deal of time.

Sam: Isn't that your job?

Sue: Yes, but not to repeat it over and over again. From now on, I am going to charge you $40 an hour for the time you keep me on the phone. That means fifteen minutes would be $10.

Sam: Boy, you're charges are high. I am going to hang up now. I have to get back to work. Thank you. Good-by.

Sue: Good-by.

In your situation, you might not be able to use the same technique Sue used, but you can use some similar technique to free yourself of the interruption from your #1 responsibility. Let people know you respect your time, and they should respect it as well.

Illustration #14

Time-Waster Check Sheet

Date	Time-Waster	Solution	Remarks

EIGHT

Decision Time-Waster Situations

"There is no time to lose."

Dennis E. Waitley

Time managers know there is only a small difference between the top leaders and the also-rans, the winners and the losers, the prepared and the unprepared managers, the people who get the promotions and the rejections. The difference is your ability to gather the decision-making information and use it successfully.

Information is critical for success. The correct decisions require factual, timely, relevant information. You must develop information-generation skills and interpreting skills to make decisions which count at home and the office. Information is available from your assistant, your associate, your boss, your local library, publications, books, governmental sources, and trade associations. Choose the correct amount of information for your needs. You must manage your information, and by doing so, you manage your time.

#149 Time-Waster: Not using your key personnel—your secretary

The scene is set: you're running around trying to get the important job done for your boss. You look out your door only to see your secretary in the middle of a huge yawn, looking completely bored. Do you know why? You are not delegating enough work. Your secretary is an important resource for helping you in your job. Use his or her talents more. Let's look at how you can do it.

Solution: Make a list of the jobs you would like to complete. Now make a list of the most important jobs your secretary or assistant performs for you. Do you assign enough work to your secretary of assistant? Do you discuss your top priorities and assignments with the people close to you? Call your secretary into your office and assign her a small job that will help you in a major job you're working on each day. When your secretary completes it successfully, thank him/her and assign another one. Release some of your work. Set up a time each day to go over the workload, and assign some work accordingly. By delegating more work, you help others feel like they are an important part of the team.

#150 Time-Waster: Failing to use the information available from your subordinates

If you have people working for you, they have an untapped resource that you can use. Since you have formal authority, you have status and access to information. You can only know so much; you need the brain power and experience of others around you.

Solution: Use the technique used by Franklin D. Roosevelt. He would use competition to gather the necessary information. He would call you into his office and ask you to find information on a particular question. When you returned with the answer, you found he already knew the answer. After he did this to you once or twice, you became very careful about your information. Be willing to demand precise information. When you get this information, you will be in a better position to use it to your benefit.

#151 Time-Waster: Unwillingness to really get to know others

Solution: A recent study of very successful general managers found that many engage in discussions with associates, customers, vendors, and others to gather important information to make decisions. These daily discussions result in a very close and rewarding atmosphere. The general managers get information to make better use of their time and make their organization a better place to work.

Here is a description of a reasonably typical day in the life of a successful executive. The individual in this case is Michael Richardson, the president of an investment management firm.

A.M.

7:35   He arrives at work after a short commute, unpacks his briefcase, gets some coffee, and begins a "To Do" list for the day.

7:40   Jerry Bradshaw, a subordinate, arrives at his office, which is right next to Richardson's. One of Bradshaw's duties is to act as an assistant to Richardson.

7:45   Bradshaw and Richardson converse about a number of topics. Richardson shows Bradshaw some pictures he recently took at his summer home.

8:00   Bradshaw and Richardson talk about a schedule and priorities for the day. In the process, they touch on a dozen different subjects and issues relating to customers and subordinates.

8:20   Frank Wilson, another subordinate, drops in. He asks a few questions about a personnel problem and then joins in the ongoing discussion. The discussion is straightforward, rapid, and occasionally punctuated with humor.

8:30   Fred Holly, the chairman of the firm and Richardson' boss, stops in and joins in the conversation. He asks about an appointment scheduled for eleven o'clock and brings up a few other topics.

8:40   Richardson leaves to get more coffee. Bradshaw, Holly, and Wilson continue their conversation.

8:42   Richardson comes back. A subordinate stops in and says hello. The others leave.

8:43   Bradshaw drops off a report, hands Richardson instructions that go with it, and leaves.

8:45   Joan Swanson, Richardson's secretary, arrives. They discuss her new apartment and arrangements for a meeting later in the morning.

8:49   Richardson gets a phone call from a subordinate who is returning a call from the day before. They talk primarily about the report Richardson just received.

8:55   He leaves his office and goes to a regular morning

meeting run by a subordinate. About thirty people are there. Richardson reads during the meeting.

9:09   The meeting is over. Richardson stops one of the people there and talks to him briefly.

9:15   He walks over to the office of one of his corporate counsels. His boss, Holly, is there, too. They discuss a phone call the lawyer just received. While standing, the three talk about possible responses to a problem. As before, the exchange is quick and includes some humor.

9:30   Richardson goes back to his office for a meeting with the vice-chairman of another firm (a potential customer and supplier). One other person, a liaison with that firm, also attends the meeting. The discussion is cordial. It covers many topics, from their products to U.S. foreign relations.

9:50   The visitor and the liaison leave. Richardson opens the adjoining door to Bradshaw's office and asks a question.

9:52   Richardson's secretary comes in with five items of business.

9:55   Bradshaw drops in, asks a question about a customer, and then leaves.

9:58   Frank Wilson and one of his people arrive. He gives Richardson a memo and then the three talk about the important legal problem. Wilson does not like a decision that Richardson has tentatively made and urges him to reconsider. The discussion goes back and forth for twenty minutes until they agree on the next action and schedule it for nine o'clock the next day.

10:35   They leave. Richardson looks over papers on his desk, then picks one up and calls Holly's secretary regarding the minutes of the last board meeting. He asks her to make a few corrections.

10:41   His secretary comes in with a card for a friend who is sick. He writes a note to go with the card.

10:50   He gets a brief phone call, then goes back to the papers on his desk.

11:03   His boss stops in. Before Richardson and Holly begin to talk, Richardson gets another call. After the call, he tells his secretary that someone didn't get a letter he sent and asks her to send another.

11:05   Holly brings up a couple of issues, and then Bradshaw comes in. The three start talking about Jerry Phillips, who has become a difficult problem. Bradshaw leads the conversation, telling the others what he has done during the last few days regarding this issue. Richardson and Holly ask questions. After a while, Richardson begins to take notes. The exchange, as before, is rapid and straightforward. They try to define the problem and outline possible alternative next steps. Richardson lets the discussion roam away from and back to the topic again and again. Finally, they agree on a next step.

P.M.
12:00   Richardson orders lunch for himself and Bradshaw. Bradshaw comes in and goes over a dozen items. Wilson stops by to say that he has already followed up on their earlier conversation.

12:10   A staff person stops by with some calculations Richardson had requested. He thanks her and has a brief, amicable conversation.

12:20   Lunch arrives. Richardson and Bradshaw go into the

conference room to eat. Over lunch they pursue business and nonbusiness subjects. They laugh often at each other's humor. They end the lunch talking about a potential major customer.

1:15   Back in Richardson's office, they continue the discussion about the customer. Bradshaw gets a pad, and they go over in detail a presentation to the customer. Then Bradshaw leaves.

1:40   Working at his desk, Richardson looks over a new marketing brochure.

1:50   Bradshaw comes in again; he and Richardson go over another dozen details regarding the presentation to the potential customer. Bradshaw leaves.

1:55   Jerry Thomas comes in. He has scheduled for the afternoon some key performance appraisals, which he and Richardson will hold in Richardson's office. They talk briefly about how they will handle each appraisal.

2:00   Fred Jacobs (a subordinate of Thomas) joins Richardson and Thomas. Thomas runs the meeting. He goes over Jacobs' bonus for the year and the reason for it. Then the three of them talk about Jacobs' role in the upcoming year. They generally agree and Jacobs leaves.

2:30   Jane Kimble comes in. The appraisal follows the same format as for Fred Jabobs. Richardson asks a lot of questions and praises Kimble at times. The meeting ends on a friendly note of agreement.

3:00   George Houston comes in; the appraisal format is repeated again.

3:30   When Houston leaves, Richardson and Thomas talk briefly about how well they have accomplished their objectives in the meetings. Then they talk briefly about some of Thomas' other subordinates. Thomas leaves.

3:45   Richardson gets a short phone call. His secretary and Bradshaw come in with a list of requests.

3:50   Richardson receives a call from Jerry Phillips. He gets his notes from the eleven o'clock meeting with Phillips. They go back and forth on the phone, talking about lost business, unhappy subordinates, who did what to whom, and what should be done now. It is a long, circular, and sometimes emotional conversation. Near the end, Phillips is agreeing with Richardson on the next step and thanking him.

4:55   Bradshaw, Wilson, and Holly all step in. Each is following up on different issues that were discussed earlier in the day. Richardson briefly tells them of his conversation with Phillips. Bradshaw and Holly leave.

5:10   Richardson and Wilson have a light conversation about three or four items.

5:20   Jerry Thomas stops in. He describes a new personnel problem and the three of them discuss it. More and more humor starts coming into the conversation. They agree on an action to take.

5:30   Richardson begins to pack his briefcase. Five people briefly stop by, one or two at a time.

5:45   He leaves the office.

Footnote: They spend most of their time with others. The average GM spends only twenty-five percent of his working time alone, and this is spent largely at home, on airplanes, or while commuting. Few spend less than seventy percent of their time with others, and some spend up to ninety percent of their time this way. *Harvard Business Review,* Nov/Dec 1982, p. 156.

This description of Richardson's day gives you a vivid description of the way he delicately weaves his time between people, places, and things to get the job done. A large part of his day is spent dealing with people, and he must be willing to get to know others in order to accomplish his goals. The more you know about others, the easier it will be to work with them. Try to become more interested in others as well.

#152 Time-Waster: Lack of emotion

Far too many people float through their workday, secretly hoping that no difficult job comes their way that day. They hope they can complete their work with a minimum of effort. The world of work can no longer afford to pay people for doing the minimum; they want employees who are excited about their work, their company, and the product or service they are trying to produce.

Solution: Get excited about yourself. Get excited about your job. Get excited about your company or organization. Whatever the project or assignment, there is a way to get it done. When people work together as a group, their total talents can be used to get the job done.

I attended a small business seminar recently, and during a group project exercise, they split the whole seminar into groups, giving each group a 8" by 16" manila envelope filled with numerous items—pencils, rubber bands, cardboard, and other office supplies. The object of the group project was to get each group to discuss the various parts, and assemble them into a product that could be sold to the general public. After taking some time to work on this project, each group would send a few representatives to present their product to the whole class.

I noticed that in each group a few people would get excited about the seminar project and work very hard to accomplish the goal. They looked at each piece to see where it could go. While others in the group would make a small effort and then begin to talk personally among themselves. The majority of the group was willing to let a small handful of people put the complete project together. Why let others do it for you? You have the ability to accomplish the job or project. Why not take a chance, even if people laugh at your final result. Some of the most successful people in the world are people that were laughed at when they first came up with their original idea. Be willing to get your body and mind excited about the job at hand.

#153 Time-Waster: Not using your time with long-term results in mind

Where do you spend your time? Your job is to find the high-payoff jobs and then put your time net around them. Far too often the time net captures the routine work, the work that should be done by your assistants, or work that you enjoy, but lacks the necessary return on time invested. Since you only get a limited amount of time nets in your lifetime, you want to make them count.

Solution: Each day carefully think about what is important to do that day. You have a huge time net. It looks like a butterfly net, and you want to use it wisely. In your personal and working life, there are numerous butterflies. Some butterflies represent very important projects. These butterflies are special, with multicolors and unique characteristics. They also have the ability to fly very high to know their territory, and they do not want to be held captive. None of the butterflies are easy to catch, but the difficult ones will require every ounce of energy and time if you are to reach them.

It will be very easy and tempting to chase the routine work butterfly, or the complaining butterfly, or the personal talk butterfly, and use your valuable time nets on them. When you use your valuable time nets, you may find yourself without a net to catch the important butterfly. When your boss gives you the annual performance appraisal, you will bring your jar of various butterflies and tell your boss about how hard you worked, sweated, crawled under brush, and repaired your nets to capture these elusive butterflies. Let's listen to the conversation:

Boss:　　　　It's good to see you. Oh, I see you brought your jar of butterflies. Let's see what you have.

You:　　　　Yes, the yellow one represents the routine work I do for you.

Boss:　　　　Oh, really, I can get any butterfly catcher for that one.

You:　　　　The orange one represents the time I spend choosing the color of our office, and the wallpaper, and the light fixtures.

Boss:　　　　That butterfly is really not too important to me.

You:　　　　I'm sorry, but I spent a good deal of time to catch these butterflies; my nets were repaired a number of times, and I needed to go to great lengths to reach them.

Boss:　　　　Are you sure you don't have any unusual, distinct butterflies with you? I really expected more from you.

You:　　　　You're not happy with my butterflies? Why not?

Boss:　　　　To be frank with you, I hired you to manage your department, and your inventory of butterflies shows me you really did not manage, but performed routine work that many others in your office can do.

You:　　　　Maybe you're right. I never looked at it that way.

Boss:　　　　During the next year, I expect to find more distinct butterflies that can help us become a better company, more competitive and more profitable in the future.

You: I will do my best.

This annual performance appraisal shows you that the amount of butterflies is not as important as the color, variety, and distinctness of the butterflies caught. Choose the butterfly, then take the time to capture it. You can do it!

#154 Time-Waster: Not paying others back

You asked your supervisors for the production information last month, and told them you would give them a copy of the report on revising the production department. You put the information away, and the report is still unfinished.

Solution: Use the information you request. When you promise a report, try to finish and distribute it as soon as possible. Your associates will give you information when they know you will use it. Develop a reputation for handling information with timeliness, efficiency and gratitude.

#155 Time-Waster: Giving in to the demands of others

The customer is always right. You must help everyone. You must be willing to help everyone in your office. The clock hands turn while you try to figure out the best ways to handle all demands around you. Why permit others to tie you in knots? Why not push the request back at your requester? Let's look at some of these methods.

Solution: Examine the request before you do anything. What is the request? Why did he/she request you to do it? Do you have to do it? Why not turn the tables around? Let's see how Betty handles this situation:

Roger:	Betty, I need delivery of 1,000 units of product A immediately.
Betta:	Oh, I would like to handle this for you, but we usually need a few days.
Roger:	I really need the shipment to keep up our production.
Betta:	Could you send your truck to pick it up?
Roger:	Yes, I think we could arrange that.
Betta:	Send your truck tomorrow around 4:00 P.M. and we will handle it.

Notice what happened here. Betty followed up the request for instant delivery by making a request of her own. Since Roger wanted instant delivery, he was willing to send his truck, and this made it much easier on Betty's time management and organization. Don't make the mistake of giving into all the demands of others.

#156 Time-Waster: Excessive newspaper reading

George H. buys the local paper each morning. As soon as he clears his desk, he begins to read it. He seems to spend time behind the paper while everything else is going on around him. Some of his associates feel that George isn't really interested in them or the organization. Some people feel that the whole world is going by while George hides behind his paper.

Solution: Reading the paper is an important function to keep up with the latest developments in the news, and the developments in your field. This can be a major time-waster if you permit it. One manager from Michigan, Paul G., a certified public accountant, reads the paper while eating breakfast—and does not read it for the rest of the day. He skims it for important business news and cuts out any important clippings for future reference. Try not to let the newspaper get in the way of important priorities.

#157 Time-Waster: Too much information

You accepted a new assignment to find new methods to save energy costs in your organization. You contact many sources from trade associations, utility companies, and the government. The mail is full each day, filling your in-box and desk.

Solution: Stop gathering information when you have enough for your assignment. Too much information can sap your time and energy.

#158 Time-Waster   Waiting for your boss to give you instructions

You know what you want to do to finish that job, but you need some information from your boss to finish it. Why wait until the boss is available to help you? Find some additional work to do until you get a chance to talk to the boss.

Solution: Be willing to make some decisions about your work. If you were the boss, would you do the job? If you owned the business, how would you do the job? Ask yourself what is the quickest, easiest way to do it. Be willing to face the job alone, and take the responsibility to do the job your way. Be willing to be a good time manager and a confident person by building your confidence day-by-day with healthy doses of new decisions. Don't wait for your boss. Do the things that are essential to do; work on your top-priority.

#159 Time-Waster: Waiting for your car at the garage

Solution: Drop your car off in the morning. Pick it up after work.

#160 Time-Waster: Looking for supplies

You know what you want to do, but once you start the job, you're forced to stop to look for the necessary supplies to finish it.

Solution: Make sure you have the necessary office supplies or the material before you start the job. Make an inventory of your supplies, and order other supplies you will need. One time manager from Canada takes an inventory of the supplies used by another successful manager; it gives her ideas for the supplies to order.

#161 Time-Waster: Accepting incomplete telephone messages

Your secretary or a member of your family gives you a telephone number, but forgot to get the full name of the caller. You have a telephone number, but it will be up to you to get the correct name.

Solution: Give instructions to your assistant or others who take your telephone calls to get the name, number, and the subject of each call. Another option for the individual who spends a good deal of time on the road is to consider installing a telephone answering machine to take messages while you're out of the office.

#162 Time-Waster: Overloading your assistant with work

Sue delegated excessive work to her assistant Bill during the last two weeks. Bill tried hard, but the excessive work made him so nervous he threatened to quit his job. Sue cannot afford to lose Bill. He is an excellent worker.

Solution: Keep a close watch on your assistants, demanding they tell you when the workload is getting too heavy so you can make the necessary adjustments. Monitor their work for timeliness, quality, and quantity regularly. Your assistants can help you keep things under control especially when you show you care about them.

#163 Time-Waster: Worrying about tomorrow

Solution: Today is all you have to deal with. Concentrate all your efforts on what you want to do today. Do what you do best today. Finish whatever you start today. Good time-management means putting yourself in motion to do the things that will give you the high-payoff results. At the end of the day, you can begin planning what you want to do tomorrow. Today is everything. Use it.

#164 Time-Waster: Excessive daydreaming

Solution: Try to use your daydreaming creatively, to come up with newer and better ideas to do your work. Daydream about the things you would like to do and see yourself doing those things. Excessive daydreaming without action will trip you into the time trap and waste your valuable time. Be your own best time manager by permitting yourself to daydream, but by putting the daydreaming to work. Try the idea you dreamed about.

Don't just talk about it. Do it and make your time pay off for you.

#165 Time-Waster: Lack of regular evaluations and feedback to others

A large air shipping company needed help when their profits dropped and losses grew larger and larger. Many suggestions were made, from hiring more people to a complete restructuring. They decided to develop goals for their employees and to review the work of each in comparison to the goal. When an employee reaches his/her goal, the supervisor offers congratulations. When the employee reaches eighty percent, the supervisor will say, "You reached eighty percent of your goal; keep it up." All employees from the truck drivers to telemarketing specialists to computer operators, were involved in this program. The employees enjoyed having a goal and receiving positive feedback when they came close to or reached it. Positive reinforcement is giving someone praise, a favorable response to their efforts, and encouraging signals that you care for them.

Solution: Make the extra effort to pat that special person on the back. Let him/her know their efforts have not been in vain. Don't make the mistake Katie V., a divisional manager for a retail dress company, made recently. She had a hard-working crew in one store, and for too long took them for granted. She never gave them any reinforcement, and often told them she could easily find others to take their jobs. Her very capable crew took this treatment for a while, but as soon as the economy turned strong, the whole crew left the store for other jobs. Katie was left by herself to hire a whole new crew to run the store. When one of the most capable and very dependable employees, Jan L., gave her notice to leave, Katie showed great surprise and began to tell her how much she was appreciated and how she would be missed. Prior to the termination notice, Katie never once showed any appreciation or took the time to tell Jan that she appreciated her. Katie spent her time in many areas, but neglected the most important area—to cultivate a caring attitude between her workers and herself. If Katie had shown a genuine interest in Jan L., she might have stayed. Good time managers are there not only for themselves but for others. People want to feel needed. People want to feel their efforts are recognized. People want to feel that their ideas count. Take the time to tell others you care.

#166 Time-Waster: Failing to use existing information

Solution: Gerry G. is a marketing research manager for an advertising agency. When Gerry begins a new marketing research assignment, he asks this important question: "Did we do a study like this in the past?" Use your current information to save time, money, and a great deal of effort.

Illustration #15

	Time-Waster Check Sheet		
Date	*Time-Waster*	*Solution*	*Remarks*

NINE

Communication Time–Waster Situations

"Why, when I am talking, does time seem to fly...."

Bob Grant

Your time is filled by both oral and written messages in and out of your organization. You must communicate to people around you. The difficult job is to spend the time necessary to communicate your message, make sure others understand it, and then return to the other important aspects of your job. Let's look at some of the communication time-wasters.

#167 Time-Waster: Repeating your message over and over again

Solution: On a Monday morning, you are sorting your three days of mail while drinking your coffee. The phone rings to tell you that your assistant cannot get his car started, and perhaps he cannot get to work today. To make it through the day, you will have to communicate successfully. Theresa W. had a formula for communicating to others. It is called TEA. This word is posted above her telephone. Let's see how she uses it when she receives the call that her assistant might not be in today.

Tell: Claire, my assistant, Bill B., will not be in today.

Explain: He has car problems

Action: Requested Claire to take over Bill's duties.

The message was clear, and Theresa used the TEA formula very well. She told Claire the situation, explained the situation, and quickly took action. A few minutes later, Theresa received a call about the air conditioner going out on the production floor. The radio weather forecaster said this day would be one of the hottest since 1900. Theresa used the TEA formula again.

Tell: The plant manager informs me the air conditioner is out.

Explain: The temperature is almost 85 degrees in production.

Action: Get it fixed immediately.

Be willing to communicate directly to the people around you. If they ask questions, be willing to answer them, and then move on to other things. Give the impression that you have other pressing things to do and they must move on to their obligations.

#168 Time-Waster: Excessive letter writing

Do you spend more time answering requests and sometimes simple questions. The cost to write one letter is over $30. Why spend your valuable time, especially, your prime time (9:00 A.M. - 6:00 P.M.) doing routine letter writing.

Solution: There are three basic ways to cut letter writing to a minimum:

1. Make a telephone call to answer the question.
2. Answer the letter on the sender's original letter in your own handwriting and mail back to him.
3. Delegate the letter writing to an assistant or someone in your office with time to do it.
4. Use a form letter book.

Write only the essential letters, the letters that need your personal direction and control. Avoid the letter writing trap; it will steal too much of your time and effort.

#169 Time-Waster: Not telling the truth, to get around a difficult situation

If you don't tell the truth, you will have to explain it completely, and this will cause you to spend much more time stretching the truth. Once you stretch the truth, you will find it very difficult to remember just what you said and when you said it; and eventually you will get caught at it.

Solution: Tell the truth. One business owner got himself in some real difficulties when he told various stories about others. He also did not give truthful information to his secretary, and it was difficult and embarrassing for the secretary to deal with untruthfulness.

Be willing to focus on the truth. You will find it much easier to remember things and you will cut stress to a minimum if you tell the truth and demand the truth from others.

#170 Time-Waster: Not listening to people complain

No one likes to listen to complaints. Some people are habitual complainers and do so whenever they get a chance. In management, in selling, at home, you must be willing to deal with these complainers, or they will consume a great deal of your time.

Solution: Be willing to listen to their complaint. Hear it out. Once you hear it, be willing to make a decision to act on the complaint now or take some time to think about it. Tell the complainer of your decision. In selling, listening to the customer's complaints can bring more knowledge about their needs and a better chance of selling them additional goods or services. Lynn G., an owner of a hand-crafted lamp company, sells primarily at craft shows. When customers walk up to her lamp table, they say many things to try to discourage the possible sale. Let's listen:

Customer:	I really like this lamp shade, but it will not fit the base. Nothing ever fits.
Lynn G.:	This an attractive shade, it will fit; it can be screwed to the base very easily.
Customer:	Oh, really, they can go together.
Lynn G.:	Yes, I can wrap it for you right now.
Customer:	I'm not sure I have the time to wait for it right now.

Lynn G.:   It will only take a few minutes to wrap it. You can take it home today.

Customer: Yes, I'll take it.

Once Lynn G. listened to the complaint, she went right to work to satisfy the customer. In some cases the customer makes up complaints or obstacles to remove themselves from buying. They really want the salesperson to say, "No, we don't have that style, size, or shape." Once you listen and then react to it you will have a much better chance of making the sale. Take the time to listen to the complaint. You can learn from it. But then take some action that will benefit your company or organization.

#171 Time-Waster: Not keeping your mailing list updated

When you do a mailing, you will find that more and more people move each year. Statistics show that people move at least five to six times during their lifetimes. Why try to keep a mailing list up to date manually?

Solution: If you have a large customer list, put it on a computer disk so you can keep it up to date. When someone moves away, change their address to the new one. The post office will give you the new address if you state this request on your outside envelope. Some people will send a mailing first class so that all undelivered mail is returned to them, and they can make any necessary additions, deletions, or corrections. Keep your mailing list updated daily to keep it current.

#172 Time-Waster: Excessive time and effort to communicate

Review the letters you have written during the past few

months. Can you find excessive wordage, excessive phrases, and redundancies? Even if you have written this way for years, you can cut it to a minimum.

Solution: Break the message down to the bare essentials. What is the basic message? Cut down on all the explaining, and deliver just the essentials of the message. Below you will find a letter written by a time-waster who wants you to believe the difficulty of his job. The subject of the letter is to notify you that he received your resume for a teaching position.

"The long-winded letter."

> ABC Community College
> 10 Oak Street
> Wills, New York 12000

December 10, 1999

Ms. Wilma Smith
7 Rose Avenue
St. Louis, MO 63100

Dear Ms. Smith:

Thank you for submitting your resume and for your interest in the full-time Business Administration faculty position at ABC Community College. A copy of the job description is enclosed. Your application is already on file in the Personnel Office.

If you have any questions on the job description, call Mr. Jefferson Davis in our personnel office by 3:00 P.M. each weekday.

Your qualifications will be reviewed and you will be advised of your status.

Your continued interest in this College is greatly appreciated.

Sincerely,

(Mrs.) Louise Carricker
Personnel Assistant

Enclosure

Here is how you could cover the basic material in the above letter, using a great deal less information.

Dear Sir:

Thank you very much for your resume. You will be given every consideration for the faculty position.

You will be contacted for an interview if we feel your background and experience meet our needs. Thank you very much for your interest.

Sincerely,

Merle Backrach
Personnel Assistant

Cut your letter to the minimum, without sacrificing the basic message you want to deliver. Use it; you will find it will work for you.

#173 Time-Waster: Poor listening skills

Your wife is giving you instructions on how to use the new stove, since she will be working late tonight. You're thinking about something else. As you drive out of your driveway on your way to work, you know you're not quite sure how to operate the stove. Why didn't you listen? Your assistant is explaining why he didn't finish an important job. You listen somewhat, but you're thinking about your upcoming meeting with your boss, and by the end of the conversation, you really don't know why your assistant didn't finish the job.

Solution: Listening is hard work. You must make an intense effort to learn this skill. One manager from Illinois found that listening was one of his most difficult skills, until he developed a CIRS formula. The steps of successful listening are:

1. Concentrate on the speaker. Look him/her in the eye.
2. Interpret what is being said.
3. Respond to show that you're listening.
4. Summarize. Show the speaker you know what he just said. Summarize the key points.

Let's listen to a time manager using this CIRS formula.

You: (Looking directly at Sue) What did you mean by that?

Sue: What, you're not listening to me? I explained how to make the entry and asked you if it was correct?

You: I understand fully. You want to know how to handle the cost for the new truck.

Sue: Yes, that's right.

You: I will get the numbers from the computer and put them together for you. Is that fair to you?

Sue: Yes. Thank you very much.

#174 Time-Waster: Not letting your workers evaluate you

Policies on the college level required all instructors to pass out student evaluations to all students, so they could give their opinions on the quality of the content and instructor's ability to teach the course. Many instructors were upset when the policy started, but now they tolerate it and find this information can make them better instructors. In your job, you can pass out a performance evaluation to your workers to get valuable feedback on your performance. No one in business knows you better than the people who work with you each day.

Solution: People want to express their opinions. The evaluation will tell you about the things they like about the job, any duplication of effort in various departments, if they feel like a member of the team, if they feel a career path is open to them, if you communicate to them enough, and if you treat them with fairness. Accept criticism, especially if it will help you.

#175 Time-Waster: Thinking the sun rises and falls on your every move

Ted M. is a very conscientious worker who has built a small business in South Dakota. He wants very much to please his customers, and when some small thing goes wrong, he gets unusually mad and stays that way all day long. This behavior upsets everyone around him. It's getting to the point where he makes his customers uneasy, and little by little he is losing some long-time and much valued customers and employees. Ted must be willing to meet himself halfway to put himself and his work situation in its proper perspective.

Solution: Don't think the sun rises and falls on your every move. Don't expect that everything should turn out just the way you want it. Your work is important, but why over-emphasize it and permit the pressure to build up. When you relax, others will relax around you. In my college classes, when I feel good about myself, I find my students begin to feel the same way. When you're nervous, upset, and trying to do too many things at once, it puts a great deal of pressure on the people around you. Don't permit the big project to overwhelm you. Break it down into as many pieces as possible, and do one piece at a time. Once you gain confidence about completing one part of the project, the others will fall into line. You will be on your way to completing it.

Ted M. must be willing to take a serious look at himself. He must be wiling to ask himself if it is him or the job. Why is he so nervous and upset all the time? High quality work is important, but perhaps Ted is expecting too much from others around him. Ted must be willing to smile more, no matter how hard it hurts, and slow down to a livable pace. He must be willing to expect obstacles along the way, and work to get around them. Flexibility helps you keep up to the demands of your job and responsibilities.

#176 Time-Waster: Using the same methods to communicate

You may communicate successfully with your family or your immediate friends, but by trying to use these techniques to communicate to others may fail because the techniques are inappropriate.

Solution: Be willing to show and tell your story. Give examples. Show graphs and signs. Write the important points on a bulletin board or blackboard. Research on communications shows that when you tell someone something, within three days a large percentage is forgotten. On the other hand, when you show and tell, a much larger percentage of your message is recalled in two or three days. Try new techniques of communication to help others understand you. When you reach your audience, they will work harder on your behalf, because they understand what you want.

Bob V., a teacher of psychology at a community college, uses a unique method to show his students the concept of personality. He shows up wearing a mask for the class, showing his students that many of us appear much differently then we really are. This class enjoys the class and gains a new understanding of the personality concept. Use various ideas to communicate your thoughts better to your audience. Pass out information to further communicate your idea. Answer any questions at the end of your talk.

#177 Time-Waster: Passing out information just prior to your talk

The annual sales meeting just started and you want to talk about the creative use of the computer and the scientific use of telemarketing in selling. You pass out the written material just prior to your talk, and you talk to fifty bowed heads trying to read your written materials.

Solution: Do not do anything to dilute maximum attention at the beginning of your talk. If you wish to pass out the information, you can do it after the body of your talk to further explain your position or procedure. Use the opening moments of your talk to fully prepare your audience for the rest of your talk.

#178 Time-Waster: Neglecting to ask or answer questions fully

When you meet with one person or talk to fifty people, you must be willing to answer their questions to fully communicate your message. The questions left unanswered will serve as the stumbling blocks of misunderstanding and waste valuable time later.

Solution: Ask your listeners to ask questions. Site examples of how you had questions from other groups and how time and effort were saved by the quick and accurate answers to the questions. There is no such thing as a simple or foolish question. When you answer the questions, try to restate the question in your own words and then answer it. When you finish the answer, ask the questioner if you answered the question to their satisfaction. Once you answer a question, move on to the next question. Thank everyone for their attention, time, and questions at the end of your talk.

#179 Time-Waster: Underestimating how you can communicate nonverbally

Your nonverbal cues are your smiles, responses, appearances of favorable attitudes, friendliness, understanding, and interest. These cues can be favorable or unfavorable for you. Sue Normand, the vice-president of a large diaper manufacturing company, is well known for her intense concentration, during which she is virtually unaware of her surroundings. Sue met for fifteen minutes with the president at the start of the morning to discuss and plan operational matters. Unfortunately, at this time Ms. Normand's head was filled with technical matters and she walked through the plant in a virtual haze of concentration. Because of this concentration, her answers to greetings from employees seemed to be more growls than a voice, and her apparently hostile outlook scared people; after all, she was "the boss."

Sue's nonverbal communication bowled people over; they hid, as best they could, as they saw her approach. The lucky ones suddenly took their coffee breaks or smoke breaks, or visited the medical department for checkups. The not-so-lucky ones merely became extremely busy on the opposite side of their machines.

Sue's nonverbal communication inaccurately communicated hostility and displeasure, which was just the opposite of

Sue's real self. She was really an outgoing person who enjoyed and like people a great deal. Her nonverbal communications were eloquently erroneous.

Solution: Be willing to break down the seriousness of your relations at work. Don't take things personally— not everyone will like you—but if you show a genuine interest in others, and you smile and feel good about yourself, you will give an important nonverbal signal to others. examine how others around you communicate to you on a nonverbal basis. Be willing to express positive nonverbal signals to reach others.

#180 Time-Waster: Avoiding communication opportunities

You know you should try to see your supervisors more often. You know you should try to give them reinforcement more often so they can feel better about themselves, but you have your own problems, your own #1's, and you're in the middle of some heavy office politics.

Solution: Successful people find a way to communicate to others around them. They seem to always have time. They make an effort to squeeze in the time, or they take the opportunity to communicate when it arrives. The opportunity to communicate might come during the weekly staff meeting, it might be in the cafeteria during lunch, or it might be at the company gymnasium. Try to establish routines, so that each employee will be contacted for individual conversation at fairly frequent intervals. By contacting them on a regular basis, you're really saying to them they count and you're willing to listen to them.

A president of a large community college, John D., gives his staff an opportunity to communicate to him by offering lunch meetings, in which a small group of people discuss their ideas, interests, and attitudes with the president. The president finds that these meetings give him a great deal of input about his staff, gives him an opportunity to meet many people directly, and develop a personal understanding about others.

#181 Time-Waster: Using words people don't understand

You feel you will impress the new employees or your associates when you use words that are difficult to understand. You seldom use these words yourself, so that when you try to use them you tend to mispronounce them, and the lines on the brows of your audience increase as you increase the use of these difficult-to-understand words.

Solution: Use words to communicate, not to confuse others. Use words that people understand. Avoid management jargon, even to other managers. Cross out the words that have many meanings. Use words that inform. One sales manager, Mae M. of Florida, will review her sales or meeting presentation with her ten-year-old daughter, and when Mae is convinced her daughter understands the message, she delivers it to her audience. Be willing to open the curtains of clarity by using only words that make your meaning clear. Take questions at the end of your talk to make certain that you're understood.

#182 Time-Waster: Talking about something you're not sure about

You promised the accounting instructors a training lesson on the use of computers in the classroom. You wanted to get Louise M. to make the presentation, but at the last minute she broke her leg during a skiing trip. You decided that you must manage the presentation, so you put together a presentation at the last minute. This is not your field, but you plow on, hoping that your efforts will succeed. You put on the presentation, but it had only moderate success, and it was a real time-waster for you. You didn't feel that you received your return on investment of your time.

Solution: Talk about only the things you know about. If you have experienced something, be willing to talk about it. No one is going to question your first-hand experience, and if they do, you will have the answers for them. Successful people communicate by talking about the things they have experienced.

#183 Time-Waster: Writing to impress others

The manager spent almost all day writing out in long-hand the letter to the customer explaining the reason for the delay in shipping the latest steel casing order. The letter outlined carefully the operational procedure to produce the steel and all the related paperwork to ship it. When the letter was finally finished, it could be used in a training course on operating a steel plant. The end result was a major time-waster that swallowed up a great deal of time and effort.

Solution: Rather than trying to impress others, strive to attain clarity in your letters and communication tools. Give answers in clear, concise terms. When you try to impress your reader or listener, you may confuse him with your complicated message; and the message may have to be revised, or another call or visit may be needed to clear up the confusion.

#184 Time-Waster: Not giving yourself a communication deadline

You want to hold the meeting to discuss the economy moves in the molding department of the Acron plant. You begin to discuss the three or four major areas, and then additional questions are asked, both in and out of the subject of the meeting. You look up at the clock, and you have a long way to go and very little time to cover the material for the meeting.

Solution: At the beginning of the meeting, list the subjects you would like to cover on a sheet to distribute to the meeting members. Give each section of the meeting a time limit, and at the beginning of the meeting, tell everyone what time you would like to finish. Most groups will work within your time frame. When someone asks a silly or irrelevant question, simply tell them you cannot respond to it; you're trying to stay on the track of the subject at hand, and must move ahead. Once you set the tone, people will work to help you reach your goals.

#185 Time-Waster: Not fully considering your audience

Solution: Are you writing to the president of the tooling company, or the training director of an automobile manufacturing company, or the research director of the university hospital? Concentrate on their background and their understanding level, and then direct your message with these factors in mind. Visualize an average day for them: what are they trying to attain, what are their major problems and goals, and how can you help them achieve their goals and objectives? Focusing on your audience and their special needs will help you develop a message that will be meaningful to them and save time. For example, if you're writing to writers, you would focus on themes, concepts, ideas, characters, etc. If on the other hand you're writing to an artist, you would focus on perspective, color, balance, etc. You lean your message in the direction of their understanding. This will not happen overnight; but with persistence and a burning desire to succeed, you can do it. Keep trying.

TEN

Proper Balance Time–Waster Situations

"Time is the most valuable thing a man can spend... "

Theophrastus

#186 Time-Waster: Spreading yourself too thin

When you spread yourself too thin, something will eventually break. When you have too many irons in the fire, the fire might go out. In a recent radio interview, I talked about the individual who tries to do too many things. He tries to watch each and every detail at work, run things at home to the finest detail, and gives too much of the very little remaining time to friends, associates, or groups. Even the super-human cannot handle all of these difficult tasks. Once you develop a reputation for taking on too much work, people will find their way to you, and pour more and more work on you.

Solution: When you find yourself being too many things, rushing from one place to another, finishing this rush job to go on to another, pleasing too many people, emptying the full container and filling the empty container, do something about it. It's similar to filling the suitcase too full before going on vacation. You might be able to put a knee on the suitcase to force it shut, but once you place it into the trunk of your car, the lid will open again. Now you're back to square one. Don't overload the suitcase. Don't make the mistake of overloading your work assignment, either. Be willing to ask yourself if you're doing the most productive thing possible at this given moment? Is it doing the filing? Is it doing the fund raising for your charity? Is it helping your assistant get the latest project finished? Is it doing your expense reports?

To succeed at work, at home, and in your personal life requires the proper time and effort to make each part of your life work. The proper balance means making your time count at work; and when results are favorable, you reward yourself and others close to you. It means letting others at home and in your personal life become a part of your life. It means taking the necessary steps to avoid unrealistic promises to yourself or others, but using your time to produce the best work possible. Just as a boat, ship, plane, or automobile will travel smoother, faster, and longer once proper balance is attained, you will accomplish more in all areas of your life with the proper balance of realistic goals and the behavior to reach them. Is it the plan for the merger of departments your boss needs for the divisional meeting? Concentrate on the important work that will give you rewards. Be willing to say "No" when someone wants you to do jobs and assignments that have a lower priority than you're presently working on. Make a huge sign and display it clearly at your desk, that reads, "Do not disturb. I'm working on my #1." This will give out the not too subtle message that you don't want to be disturbed.

When you find yourself trying to do too many things, call a meeting with yourself, and drop the things, projects, assignments, and busywork which do not contribute to your #1 priority. Cut down on your meetings and appointments until the #1 priority is completed. Give yourself a reward when you finish that #1 priority. The reward might be going to a sporting event, buying a new dress, or going out to a special restaurant or play.

#187 Time-Waster: Starting many jobs, but never finishing any

The vice-president of your bank assigned you a new job. You eagerly started the job. A week later you simply added it to a couple of dozen other jobs. You filed it in your uncompleted job file and there is a good chance you will never finish any of them. But you know you will be judged for advancement and raises by your ability to finish them.

Solution: When you take on a new job, be certain that you do an adequate amount of thinking about it. Be willing to put the plans on paper and discuss it within your office, especially with people who know about your project or might know how you can gather resources on it. Work on the job until it is finished, so you can take on another job. Let's listen to the boss asking Donna (the procrastinator) about an unfinished job.

Boss: Donna, did you finish the job on our Accounts Receivable Report? I want to know who owes us money.

Donna: Not quite, but I'm working on the mailing list of foreign customers.

Boss: I wanted that foreign list a long time ago. But that

list is not my priority now. I need the Accounts
Receivable Report.

Donna: Sorry, I'm working on quite a few jobs.

Boss: I know, but I really don't care about all the other
jobs. The only one I want right now is the Accounts Receivable listing.

Donna: I'll squeeze it in for sure today.

Boss: The people who get promotions here are people
who produce jobs, on time, when assigned. I need
it immediately.

Donna: I will finish it today. You will have it by five
o'clock.

In your job, visualize your boss asking for the job you're
working on, right on the deadline, or the day before the deadline. Remember that each job correctly completed on time will
carve out a reputation on which you can build your career.
Concentrate fully on the job at hand forgetting about all future
jobs until the present one is completed. Keep a list of all completed jobs to remind your boss of them during your performance evaluation.

#188 Time-Waster: Poor office location

You want to make a decision on the new budget; it is due
next week. Since your office is located adjacent to personnel,
you're interrupted by job applicants, people asking directions,
others asking simple questions, and drop-in visitors. By the end
of the day, you're exhausted; but the important work is still in
your in-box, waiting for you to finish it.

Solution: Move your desk to a quiet area. Keep moving your desk until you find an area where you can concentrate fully. If you cannot move, spend more time away from your desk, such as a library, a conference room, an empty office, or even the desk of an employee out sick for the day or on a vacation. If all else fails, try closing the door.

#189 Time-Waster: Unrealistic promises

Kim is a customer relations supervisor for a large mail order company in Maine. She wants to give the best possible service to her customers, and makes promises that are too difficult to meet. When the promise is broken, the customer gets mad and Kim becomes stressed out. There must be a better way.

Solution: Don't fall into the trap of promising too much. When you feel it will take you three days to get the information for the customer, tell your customer four or five days is required. Many things can happen during the three days. If you can get the project done in three days, and deliver it to the customer, you become a hero. If you run into a problem, or you take a day off for sickness, you can still finish it within the five days. Promise what you can deliver.

#190 Time-Waster: Being late for work

Solution: Leave for work early enough so you will arrive in time, even when the major highway backs up, the train is delayed, or the subway breaks down.

#191 Time-Waster: Dozing off after lunch

Solution: Eat a lighter lunch. Take a brisk walk around the block after lunch. Change your work activities after lunch.

#192 Time-Waster: Dining out in a new restaurant across town, during busy periods at work

Peter V., a transportation manager with a large trucking company, called to ask you about the self-insurance program in your company. You owe Peter V. a favor, and this could be an opportunity to pay him back. You agree to meet him for lunch, across town in the new Italian restaurant. Your workload is still waiting for you when you return. Let's see how you could handle this time-waster in a better way.

Solution: The phone rings off the hook, and your work is piled high in front of you.

Peter:	I would certainly like to get together and discuss the self-insurance program with you.
You:	I certainly would like to meet with you, but, Peter, this is our busy time of year.
Peter:	I think we could wrap it up during one lunch hour. Why not?
You:	Perhaps, but not right now. We're doing the year-end work right now, and I can't spare any extra time. When things slow down, I will get back to you.
Peter:	It's all right with me. I will talk to you later.
You:	Good-by.

You have the ability to select the timing of your activities. You're the manager of your time. If you feel that certain priorities take precedence over others, be willing to say "No" when you need to say it. Let people know that your responsibilities are important. Save those dining experiences as a reward when you finish the important work related duties.

#193 Time-Waster: Signing numerous correspondences and checks

Beverly L., the office manager of a large dental equipment company, works long hours, but finds she never has time to make the decisions to run the company better. On closer examination of her workload, I found Beverly makes certain her signature is on all checks, insurance policies, and additions, and she also supervises the routine purchase of office supplies. Many of these jobs could be handled by others.

Solution: Why do you sign all the checks? Why not delegate some of the routine purchasing and routine paperwork assignments to your assistant. Save some of your valuable time and energy for the decisions necessary to run your company successfully. If you pay your employees good money, make use of their talents and abilities.

#194 Time-Waster: Failing to look at all angles of a problem

Solution: Why just assume you can handle the job or assignment when you accept it? Time managers who take the necessary time to look at all possible outcomes of a problem will be in a much better position to deal with them. Don C., a strong competitor, was captain of his high school and college football teams, and on his first job out of college, he worked his way up to the top position in one of the largest real estate management firms in Boston. His latest dream is to construct one of the biggest buildings in Boston. He received the backing of a large investment firm only when he was able to explain the potential problems as well as the potential outcomes. He was willing to look directly at the problems for all angles, and was willing to discuss them. Don did not back down, and he was awarded the money to build his building. He was able to communicate his awareness of the problems and his many ideas about how to deal with them. Don did his homework completely and received the rewards.

#195 Time-Waster: Unwillingness to change bad habits

You know you spend too much time at work, and your husband is upset with you. You spent far too much time on the golf course or at the new shopping mall looking for clothes. You watch far too much television and read fewer and fewer books. You fell into some bad habits. You want to change, but need some help.

Solution: You manage your life and what you accomplish in your life. Managing your life successfully requires an honest evaluation of the areas where you can spend your time more constructively. A good place to start will be to review the "Time-Waster Checklists" at the end of each chapter of this book. For example, Beverly is an inside sales representative for a large computer educational company, and when she read the chapter on overmanaging time-waster situations, she realized she spent too many hours on the phone directing her girlfriend's life, rather than using her work time.

Mike found that after reading the chapter on communication time-waster situations, he needed more confidence speaking to others. After reviewing his "Time-Waster Checklist," Fred decided to enroll at a local college to take a public speaking course. You manage all your activities; an important part of success is your willingness to change a bad habit into a good one.

#196 Time-Waster: Returning all phone messages yourself

Your business takes you out of your office to deal with

clients, suppliers, and the home office. When you finally get back to your office, your assistant, Fred, hands you a large stack of yellow phone messages. You get back to your desk and call each one, and the hands on the clock above your desk go wild. You just wasted two golden hours. There is a better way.

Solution: Sort the phone messages into piles. One pile should include the top-priority calls, the second pile includes important items, the third one is the low-priority calls. Now call your assistant Fred into your office, and delegate the low-priority calls to him. While Fred is in the office, go through the second pile, the important items, and see how many Fred can call for you. Instruct him to keep you posted on important information from these calls. At the same meeting with Fred, tell him to handle these calls when they come in originally, instead of making a yellow phone message.

#197 Time-Waster: Too much work at home

You job takes a tremendous amount of your time, effort, and energy. Just when you relax at home, and start to unwind, you're reminded of the numerous things that must be done around the house. The screen door needs to be fixed; it's still hanging by one side. You're tired of trying to find alibis for why you cannot fix it. The reason you neglected the door is because you started the addition to the house, and that project is taking up the bulk of your time. The housework is piling up, and you spend all weekend trying to keep it under control. You want to go out Saturday night, but you're too tired. Your life is on hold, because you're taking on too much homework, too many responsibilities that are slowing you down.

Solution: What are the essential things that must be done around the house? Do you have to do them? Can you get help from other family members? Can you hire someone to do your work? In order to meet the requirements of your job, you must examine the opportunities to get the required rest at home. To determine the amount of time and money spent in non-working activities, examine the illustration that follows. When you spend time in non-productive areas, you lose both money and energy. Fill out the chart in the illustration. Determine if you are investing your time or simply spending it. You can save a great deal of time at home by putting it to work in high-payoff and beneficial areas. You can be the manager of your time.

"How Much Time Can I Save in One Day and What's it Worth?"

Non-Selling Activity	I currently average about this many hours	Starting tomorrow I will save this many hours
Getting Ready for Work		
Eating		
Coffee Breaks		
Goofing Off		
Personal Business		
Relaxing		
Television		
Other Entertainment		
Family		
Studying		
Hobby		
Sports		
Sleeping		
Other		

Total hours I will save each day ....

Hours saved per week   weeks available

hours per year

hours per year × $ S

my hourly worth   increased earnings

By converting some of my "lost time" to productive time EACH AND EVERY day
I can add $ to my income in the next 12 months!

#198 Time-Waster: Not using one-minute praise and scoldings

Successful people know how to manage their time, but also how to keep their sanity and strength while dealing with their own priorities. They understand the benefit of working together to succeed together. They understand that if their organization can't pull together they may lose the race. Successful people know the importance of taking time to stroke people positively, so they can continue with their fine work. Roberta R. of South Dakota is the manager of a large bank who talks with all her staff members once a week, and on a one-on-one basis each month. She finds that by talking to them often, she can get a feel for their problems and concerns before they get out of hand. Let's listen while Roberta talks to Raymond B. about his outstanding record of selling I.R.A. (Individual Retirement Accounts) at the bank.

Roberta: Sit down, Ray. Nice to see you again. How is your department doing these days?

Ray: Fine, just fine. Sue is doing great on the sales desk. The volume of work is heavy this week; the customers want to take advantage of the deductions.

Roberta: Yes, I'm pleased with the figures, as well as the operation of the department. You are valuable to me, and this company needs your talents and skills more than ever.

Ray: I appreciate that very much. Say, I understand that a stress-reduction seminar will be held in the Bismark branch in March. I would really like to attend.

Roberta: Yes, I have something on it. I will look it over and get back to you with an answer. Would you be interested in presenting it to your employees when you return?

Ray: I would be happy to do it.

Notice how Roberta used positive stroking techniques to make things run smoothly. She let him know that his work is excellent and the company needs him. People want to feel important, and one way to make them feel this way is to tell them their efforts count. One very successful book tells managers to use one-minute sessions to praise and scold members of their company. Praise is like putting money into the bank; the more money you put into the bank, the larger the interest you receive. You can become a team player by doing the little things to help others achieve their goals. Do the paperwork to complete the seminar requirements, finish the quarterly sales reports, finish the journal entries, finish the little things, so you can help the whole team get things done. Manage your time by being a team player, and your results will be victory after victory.

#199 Time-Waster: Not using the latest time-management techniques

Solution: When you started your job, you raised your eyebrow when a time-management principle was broken; but now you look the other way, or even bend a time-management principle yourself. You attended all the time-management workshops when you started your job, now you're getting rusty.

Keep up to date with the latest time-management techniques by watching other successful time managers and by attending time-management seminars. Just one new idea might be worth thousands of dollars. Just by reading this book shows you're serious about the most important resource of all—TIME. You're an important role model. When you watch your time, others will notice it and keep a closer watch on their own time. Give a copy of this book as a gift to associates, colleagues, employees or customers. Remember, use only one time-management technique at a time. Once this technique becomes part of your style, you can then start on a new one.

ELEVEN

Time for Time-management

We have finished discussing the 199 basic time-wasters. It will be up to you to choose the most important time-waster or time-wasters, and to take some action. Don't make the mistake of trying to solve four or five different time-wasters at the same time. Take one at a time, and work on it for three or four weeks, until you're able to incorporate the solution of the time-waster into your normal work or lifestyle. Read the book often, and check the Time-waster Checklists. Changing behavior is difficult, but to succeed in the battle of the time clock, you must be willing to make the effort to succeed.

Successful time managers know the value of using all the resources available to them. Treat other people around you with respect. Expect and demand the best from them. If people feel you're confident about them, they will work harder to succeed. Plan ahead in all time frames, including daily, monthly, yearly, and the five-year plan. Search for the latest, most efficient ways to do your job. Read and reread this book. Use it as a future guide. Your time-wasters will change according your job, your company, your goals, and your attitude. If you act and speak like a time manager, people will follow you and participate in your goals and activities.

Time managers take the time to react and evaluate their goals. They look closely at the amount of time and effort given to the completion of those goals. They fuel their assistants and associates by motivating and rewarding them for successful and competent contributions. They strive to work on their #1 priorities. Even when they get sidetracked by the procrastinator and the pessimist, the time managers bounce back, and return to the #1 priority. But most of all, the successful time managers know how to deal with the everyday time-wasters that could strangle them each day; the telephone, the do-nothing employees, the drop-in visitors, the aggressive and time-consuming salesperson, the long meetings, the lack of daily plans, the numerous, routine questions, the excessive personal chatter and the failure to use your commuting time.

Close those time-waster traps. If you close the time-wasters, you will save your most valuable possession: YOUR TIME. You own your own time. It's up to you to spend it wisely. You have special skills, talents, and abilities; and to use them will require sufficient time to work on your goals. Be selfish about your time. Don't let others steal it. Be respectful of the time of others. Continue to ask yourself this important question: How important is the work I'm doing at this given moment? Be willing to focus your time on your goals. Fight your way out of the time-waster traps, and continue until you win. You deserve to win, because you have interest in and respect for how you manage your time.

Please send any of your favorite time-waster situations to me at the following address:

> **William Bond**
> **67 Melrose Avenue**
> **Haverhill, MA 01830**